THE
NEGOTIATION
TOOLKIT

THE NEGOTIATION TOOLKIT

How to Get Exactly What You Want in Any Business or Personal Situation

Roger J. Volkema

AMACOM

American Management Association

New York • Atlanta • Boston • Chicago • Kansas City • San Francisco • Washington, D.C.
Brussels • Mexico City • Tokyo • Toronto

Special discounts on bulk quantities of AMACOM books are available to corporations, professional associations, and other organizations. For details, contact Special Sales Department, AMACOM, an imprint of AMA Publications, a division of American Management Association, 1601 Broadway, New York, NY 10019. Tel.: 212-903-8316 Fax: 212-903-8083

This publication is designed to provide accurate and authoritative information in regard to the subject matter covered. It is sold with the understanding that the publisher is not engaged in rendering legal, accounting, or other professional service. If legal advice or other expert assistance is required, the services of a competent professional person should be sought.

Library of Congress Cataloging-in-Publication Data

Volkema, Roger J.
    The negotiation toolkit : how to get exactly what you want in any business or personal situation / Roger J. Volkema.
        p.   cm.
    Includes bibliographical references and index.
    ISBN 0-8144-8008-X
    1. Negotiation in business.   2. Negotiation.   I. Title.
    HD58.6.V65   1999
    158'.5—dc21   99-32273
                                                           CIP

Printing number

10   9   8   7   6   5   4   3   2   1

To my father,
who introduced me to my first tools.

Contents

Acknowledgments

Any work of this sort is a product not just of a single author but rather the contributions of a whole host of friends and associates who provide encouragement and advice. I would like to thank Robert Wilson, Tom Sinclair, Elmore Alexander, Harry Webne-Behrman, Patti Sinclair, Fred Niederman, Tom Bergmann, Martha Davidson, Cathy Healy, Alison Davy, and Samantha Lang, who read pieces of earlier drafts and provided editorial advice as well as support. Rob Jolles served as my mentor in navigating the publishing waters and securing a contract with AMACOM. In addition, there are countless students, managers, and executives who attended courses, workshops, and seminars I have offered over the years. Their participation and observations have been priceless. Finally, I wish to thank Ellen Kadin, my editor at AMACOM, for her guidance, and the American Management Association for its support.

Introduction

I once accompanied the treasurer of an organization to which I belonged to a bank in order to withdraw money for a fund-raising event. Needing several thousand dollars from our account, we went to a branch of the bank that was nearby but unfamiliar to either of us. When the bank representative came back to tell us that neither of our names was on the signature card to allow release of funds, the treasurer responded in a firm yet most sincere voice: "John, that just won't do. We need to have the money." It was said in a manner that cannot easily be described in words, and it propelled the representative to go back and get the money.

This book is not written for the treasurer of that organization. Rather, it is for you and me, everyday negotiators who do not come by it naturally but for whom negotiating is nevertheless an important skill.

That's the good news: Negotiation is a skill. In fact, negotiation entails a host of skills, and skills can be learned. You can acquire new tactics and alter old behaviors. To do so, however, requires insight and practice. This book contains ideas for helping you understand your strengths as a negotiator and recognize other negotiators' strategies and tactics.

But to develop new skills, you will want to practice these behaviors as often as possible. Just as with a sport such as golf— where every experienced player knows that you must relax, keep your head down, and follow through—the more you practice, the better you get at using these basic skills. With negotiation, however, you do not need to lug around a heavy bag or pay greens fees. There are countless opportunities available daily to practice negotiating.

To help you get started, this book has been written in an interactive format. That is, there are questions (and answers), self-assessments, minisurveys, and action challenges. In Chapter 3, for example, you are asked to apply the three fundamental questions of negotiation to an upcoming negotiation. In Chapter 15, you are asked to rate your comfort with and usage of specific negotiation tactics. In still other chapters, you are challenged to negotiate with a spouse, friend, or colleague. You start with simple negotiations and work up to more complex scenarios. All these activities are designed to get you to think about your knowledge, beliefs, and practices and to help you gain more confidence and experience as a negotiator.

The focus is primarily on two-party negotiations because these are the ones encountered daily. These include negotiations between you and your spouse, children, boss, friends, neighbors, coworkers, doctors, waiters, repair people, bank clerks, airline agents, retail sales clerks, government representatives, or others. Most of the fundamentals of two-party negotiation apply to more complicated negotiations involving multiple parties. Once you reach the end of the book, you will have more confidence, knowledge, and skills in your social and business negotiations.

It doesn't end with the final chapter of this book. I want to hear about your triumphs and tribulations; the new tactics you have discovered; your experiences negotiating socially as well as professionally; your cross-cultural negotiations; and any other past, present, or future negotiations that you find important, worrisome, memorable, or amusing. Feel free to contact me at my e-mail address, volkema@american.edu, and I'll be happy to respond.

One final procedural matter before you get started. This book contains everything you need to assess and improve your negotiating skills, with few exceptions. To reap full benefit from the ideas and challenges presented here (that is, to take advantage of the interaction with me and others), you will want:

- ❖ A pencil (with a good eraser)
- ❖ Three negotiating partners or opponents (a spouse, friend, or coworker) willing to help you for a total of about fifteen to twenty minutes each
- ❖ One or more people to play a fifteen-minute game of cards with you

I tried negotiating with the publisher to include all of these aids with the book, but given insurance and packaging costs for the negotiating partners, I was "persuaded" to settle for a larger advance instead. This is the strawman tactic, described in Chapter 10.

You don't need the negotiating partners right away, but you should begin thinking about who to ask to participate in this learning opportunity. Optimally, you should choose three people, to give you the experience of approaching individuals with potentially different styles. In a sense, lining up these three people is your first negotiation.

But before you become too engrossed in your search for negotiating partners or opponents, let's cover some basics. And what could be more basic than a definition of *negotiation?*

THE
NEGOTIATION
TOOLKIT

1

Understanding Negotiation

Nothing, of course, begins at the time you think it did.
—Lillian Hellman, playwright

The word *negotiation*, or a variation of it, is used or encountered in some circles almost daily. We talk about negotiating an agreement, negotiating a raise, labor-management negotiations, peace negotiations, contract negotiations, contract renegotiations. We even talk about negotiating a curve (when behind the wheel of an automobile) or an iceberg (in the case of a ship).

You have probably used the term *negotiation* (or more likely, the verb *negotiate*) within the past week, and you have probably negotiated ten or twenty times for every time you used the word in speech. How would you define *negotiation*? Write your definition below.

What Is Negotiation?

Most contemporary definitions contain four or five basic elements. They define *negotiation* as a *process*, generally consisting of *communication or interaction*. It involves *two or more parties*. These parties have *conflicting goals or interests*. The object is to reach *an agreement or reconciliation*. Your definition probably had some or all of these elements.

You may be surprised to learn the origin of the word. It

comes from the Latin *negotium*, which literally means not (*neg*) + ease or leisure (*otium*). For many of us, negotiation certainly feels like "not leisure." But in fact, "not leisure" is another way of saying "business." In ancient times, negotiation was business, and business was negotiation. Several Romance languages to this day have words revealing this connection (for example, *negocio* in Spanish means "business").

A more recent definition (from about A.D. 1425) comes from the Old French *negociacion*, undoubtedly borrowed from the Latin *negotium*, which is defined as a dealing with people. Clearly this is a much broader interpretation of the term, encompassing more than simply business transactions. All dealings between people—social or business—constitute negotiation.

As every good author should, I have my own definition, which is a cross between the Old French and contemporary definitions. To my mind, negotiation is

> Communication between two or more parties to determine the nature of future behavior

What I like about this definition, in addition to its simplicity, is that it defines *negotiation* very broadly (like the Old French). When someone pulls you into her office to give you "inside information" on a change in company policy or personnel, a negotiation has begun. When you send a résumé to a prospective employer, the quality of the paper communicates something. When you enter a room full of eligible partners, what you are wearing and how you carry yourself communicate something. (Appearance is the reason lawyers make criminal defendants dress to the nines for a day in court.) When someone hears or reads about you before a formal social introduction or business meeting occurs, a negotiation has begun.

General Colin Powell's candidacy for the U.S. presidency in 1996 is one of the best illustrations of the "reach" of negotiation. Well before the public and most of the media knew who he was, let alone where he stood on any of the issues of the day, his candidacy was creating excitement and building momentum. Not only had his reputation preceded him but his reputation had preceded his reputation! The fact that he was referred to as *General* Colin Powell was central to his emergent candidacy (recall General Washington, General Grant, and General Eisenhower, all of whom became U.S. presidents).

Negotiation is occurring all the time, whether you are physically present or not. For social creatures like us, negotiation is a process akin to and entwined with life itself. Consequently, it is useful to think of negotiation as a lifestyle rather than as isolated or discrete episodes along life's journey. It is an attitude as well as a set of behaviors, and all attitudes are communicated nonverbally as well as verbally.

Now that we've gotten the definition squared away, let's muddy the waters a bit. The title *The Negotiation Toolkit* suggests the book is a practical guide to effective negotiation in business and social situations. But people also use the terms *bargaining* or *bargaining and negotiation* in describing these behaviors. Is there a difference between bargaining and negotiation?

Many people use these terms interchangeably. When there is a distinction, *negotiation* is generally viewed as the broader concept and *bargaining* describes the process of determining the final price of a purchase or sale. Although the Blondie cartoon featuring Dagwood at his favorite greasy spoon suggests that dickering over four versus five meatballs is negotiation, it might better be labeled bargaining and seen as a facet of negotiation. Negotiation also involves the process of discovery, and multiple issues are often at stake.

Reprinted with special permission by King Features Syndicate.

I don't make the distinction between bargaining and negotiation idly. Many times people forgo the discovery process and simply bargain. They see only a single issue—often money—and they see it in fixed terms. That is, the more you receive, the less I am able to keep. One of the goals of this book is to help you see and experience the full range of opportunities available through negotiation, and to avoid moving prematurely to a bargaining orientation. More often than not, once you begin haggling over a single issue such as price, it becomes more difficult to think in broader terms and multiple issues, and to discover breakthroughs that allow all parties to get what they want.

What Is Negotiable?

An important part of negotiating is understanding, what is negotiable? Or to turn the question around, What is not negotiable? Think about it for a moment. Is there anything that is not negotiable?

Some people might argue that death is nonnegotiable. There is an old bromide: "Nothing is sure but death and taxes." It's hard to find examples of anyone negotiating the former—negotiating death. Daniel Webster was reported to have been such a skilled debater/negotiator that he could outduel the Devil, but it has never been verified. Harry Houdini, the great escape artist that he was, has yet to be sighted. Nor has the genuine Elvis.

Moreover, there are few if any accounts of prophets or others negotiating with God (although most of us have tried). No known version of the Bible, for example, records that before coming down from the mountain, Moses thanked and complemented God on the Ten Commandments, and then looked Him in the eye and said, ". . . but could we talk about number seven?"

As for the other nonnegotiable thing in life, to the surprise of many the Internal Revenue Service is not omnipotent. Thousands of people, often by way of their accountants or lawyers, have negotiated tax returns, penalties, and jail terms. One also can negotiate with banks, mortgage companies, airlines, automobile repair shops, telephone companies, waiters, credit card companies, supervisors, husbands, wives, and children. (Many take a marriage vow to "trust, honor, and obey for as long as we both shall live," yet divorce statistics clearly show that these vows too—and the religious, social, and legal codes that accompany them—are negotiable.)

Herb Cohen, in his book *You Can Negotiate Anything* (1980), contends that anything that was negotiated is negotiable. This implies that almost everything but the laws of nature (for example, the speed of light, the force of gravity on earth) is negotiable. Interest rates were negotiated, so they are negotiable. The prices of automobiles, food, housing, repair work, and clothing were all determined through some intrapersonal or interpersonal process involving facts and opinions; these are all negotiable.

Even when you have a bona fide contract, it can be renegotiated. We need to look no further than the sports page of a metropolitan newspaper to see where a baseball or football player who negotiated a record-setting, multimillion dollar, multiyear contract last year now wants to renegotiate it because another player has just signed somewhere for more money. And the team owners do it!

The critical issue here is not so much what is negotiable or not negotiable, in the absolute sense, but what you *think* is negotiable or nonnegotiable. If you consciously or subconsciously believe that something is nonnegotiable, then it might as well be so. In the previous cartoon, Dagwood had to ask for more meatballs before he could hope to get them. In reality, I have encountered people who simply do not ask for what they want, whether it is a new contract or half a glass of beverage for half the price of a full glass. This is most unfortunate, especially when both or all parties to a negotiation want the same thing but no one has the wherewithal to ask for it.

Jerry Harvey, a consultant and professor of management, writes about a worst-case scenario. A group of people, all of whom want the same thing, assume that the others want something else, and each person fails to ask for his or her true desires. As a consequence, the group takes actions that are contrary to the desires of *everybody* in the group. He calls this the Abilene Paradox, after an incident in which he and his wife and in-laws took a fifty-three mile trip to Abilene, Texas, during the peak of summer in a car without air conditioning, a trip that *none* of them wanted to take. (For more on the Abilene Paradox, see the video by the same title in the Resources section at the end of this book.)

Successful negotiation begins with the belief that almost everything is negotiable, and almost everyone will negotiate with you. Some negotiations simply require a little more creativity and panache than others.

So, let's test your mettle. The next time that you go to a restaurant (tonight, or tomorrow for lunch), look over the menu and then ask yourself what you would really like that isn't on the menu. Maybe the restaurant offers a taco salad with your choice of beef, chicken, or chili, but you would like all three. Ask for the combination. Maybe you would enjoy a cherry milkshake, but they only show vanilla and chocolate on the menu (although you know they put cherries on their sundaes). Ask them to blend some cherries into a vanilla milkshake. Perhaps you have a craving for pizza with bananas and pineapple on it, but there are no such toppings listed on the menu.

Ask for what you really want, and see if you can get it. You may have to help the waiter or waitress imagine how it can be done. But if you approach your server in a friendly, unassuming, positive manner, there is a good chance of getting what you ask for.

Choosing Not to Negotiate

It's been a long night. Bill Gates, the founder of Microsoft, is sitting around with a group of friends. They're famished. Someone gets the idea to call Domino's Pizza for a late-night delivery. The owner-manager of Domino's answers the phone, but unfortunately the store has just closed. Disappointed, the caller is ready to hang up when someone in the group says, "Tell them you're Bill Gates and pay them a lot of money to deliver a pizza." Bill Gates hesitates. "Bill," someone prods, "what's it worth to you to have a pizza?" "Two hundred forty dollars," Gates responds. He gets on the phone and says, "OK, I'm Bill Gates and I'll pay you $240 to bring this pizza." They got the pizza.

Why did Bill Gates require prodding? Is he not the great ne-gotiator we all assume him to be? Perhaps it's just that he has gotten better at negotiating (or chosen agents to represent him), since this story is set during the very early days of Microsoft. More likely, we are talking about a negotiation that simply did not mean much to him. He could take it or leave it.

Like Bill Gates, you may choose not to negotiate in a particu-lar situation. This decision can be made consciously or subcon-sciously, and for a variety of reasons. For example, you may choose not to negotiate because the issue(s) are not that impor-tant to you but they appear to be critical for the other party. On a trip through Cleveland, your spouse wants to stop and see the Rock and Roll Hall of Fame. You are not a big fan of that ol' time-a rock 'n' roll, but it seems very important to your spouse; so you agree to go along. Or, concerned about a mediocre merit evalua-tion, you may decide not to negotiate with your boss because she is very intimidating and your negotiations with her always seem to turn into win-lose arguments, with you losing. Or, perhaps in general you simply lack the will to negotiate with people and repeatedly accommodate or avoid confrontation.

These are very different motivations for not negotiating. In terms of the trip through Cleveland, you may not have strong feelings one way or the other and so you go along with your spouse's obvious desire. There may be a creative solution that gives both of you what you want (for example, you can get some-thing to eat at the coffee shop or restaurant and read the paper while your spouse tours), but looking for that win-win solution may not be worth the time and energy in this situation.

At the other end of the spectrum, you may never seem to have the energy or motivation to negotiate, because of your nego-tiation skills or your personality. It is important to be aware of this characteristic and to recognize its implications for negotiat-ing with all types of people and in all types of situations. We come back to this a bit later in the book.

Take a moment and think back about your day (or the previ-ous day, if you are reading this in the morning). Retrace the events and encounters of your day. Can you think of any situa-tions where you had an opportunity to negotiate but didn't? What were the circumstances? Why didn't you pursue your interests? Faced with a certain kind of individual or situation, do you always choose not to engage the other party in issues that are important to you?

Knowing when to negotiate and when not to is an important skill in itself. Going into a restaurant and ordering a dish that is not on the menu when the restaurant is short-staffed and your waiter is very busy, for example, may not make sense. Similarly, if you discover that the restaurant does not carry raw octopus, you either have to think of a substitute or drop your request.

On the other hand, unless you are a natural negotiator, consistent avoidance of negotiation means that you are missing opportunities to practice and hone your skills. More importantly, consistent avoidance means you are abrogating your role in determining the nature of future behavior between you and your family, you and your friends, and you and others. (Remember the use of "the nature of future behavior" in my definition?) Oftentimes, you are just prolonging the inevitable. If you are shy about asking a cab driver how much it costs to take you to your hotel, then you should be prepared to pay the driver whatever he tells you once you arrive at the hotel, because it is a lot more difficult to negotiate after the fact (unless you are prepared to walk off and pay nothing, which I do not recommend).

Ultimately, choosing when to negotiate is a personal matter. A good friend once told me that his motto was "lose a little, gain a lot." That is, he chose his battles carefully and was willing to give in on issues that mattered more to others than to him in order to gain an advantage in future negotiations that were important to him. When it comes to negotiating, here are some situations that generally warrant choosing to pass:

* The situation is physically or psychologically dangerous.
* You are too tired, sick, distracted, or confused to negotiate effectively.
* The issues are trivial or symptomatic of larger concerns.
* There are others who can negotiate these issues more effectively.
* You perceive no chance of satisfying your needs.
* The other party appears incapable of rational thinking.

- You can gain social points toward a subsequent negotiation.
- The relationship is critical to you.
- You stand to lose much more than you might gain.

You should always reserve the right not to negotiate, for any of these reasons; but our goal is to move you a little beyond your comfort zone. We begin with some basic or fundamental principles—in particular the Golden Rule of Negotiation.

2

The Golden Rule of Negotiation

It is unwise to do unto others as you would have them do unto you. Their tastes may not be the same.
— George Bernard Shaw

Don Novello is a comedian best known for his portrayal of Father Guido Sarducci, a writer (Novello tells us) for the rock and society pages of the Vatican tabloid *L'Osservatore Romano* who often subs for the Pope when his holiness cannot make an event. Dressed all in black, with a broad-brimmed hat, sunglasses, and an ever-ready cigarette, Father Guido dispenses his personal, hip interpretations of history and church doctrine with a strong Italian accent.

One of his routines concerns not the institution of religion but rather higher education. He offers a new model for education, which he calls "the Five-Minute University" (FMU). After four years (or five or six, for some of us) of college training, he asks, what do you remember? Really, what do you remember? Not very much. If you take a semester or two of Spanish, what do you remember after the course is over: *¿Como está usted?* Because this is *all* you remember, this is all that needs to be taught at the Five-Minute University. Suppose you take economics, one of the more difficult academic subjects—micro- and macroeconomics. What do you remember from all the equations, formulae, theories, assumptions, etc.: "supply and demand." That's all you remember. So that's all that is taught at the FMU, because that is all you are going to remember anyway.*

This brings us to the idea of a course on negotiation. What would they teach at the FMU? If they only had fifteen or twenty seconds, if they had to boil it down to one concept or one phrase, what would it be?

This is it. This is the essence of negotiation—the Golden Rule, if you like. If you take nothing else from this book, recognize this:

> **People will not negotiate with you unless they believe you can help them or hurt them.**

Have you ever been on a long walk and wished someone would stop and give you a ride because the heat or humidity has caught up with you? Most passing motorists won't pick up a hitchhiker; it is nonnegotiable. But on rare occasions, someone does stop and ask you for directions. If this person is going your way, suddenly you are faced with an easy negotiation (and a lift to your destination). Why? Because you are in a position to help this individual by providing directions. You can also help people by smiling, shaking their hands, congratulating them, patting them on the back, calling them by their first names, hugging them, listening to their stories, buying their used cars, etc., if this is what they need.

On the other side of the coin, people also will negotiate with you if they think you can hurt them. A representative from one of the long-distance telephone providers is likely to offer inducements to gain or retain your business if he believes you might be thinking of switching to another provider. A contractor is more likely to finish the work on your retaining wall as per specifica-

*By the way, if you are interested in an advanced professional degree at the FMU, such as a law degree, you need to devote one more minute. What do they teach at the FMU law school? "Never ask a question to which you do not already know the answer." The FMU medical school requires an additional minute as well, during which you are taught "First, do no harm." But there is also a residency requirement.

tions if he or she has not yet been paid and believes this work could influence payment. A supervisor is likely to hear your concerns or complaints if she believes you might otherwise be less productive, spread ill will throughout the department, or go to a higher-up with your grievance. (In an episode from his popular TV sitcom, Jerry Seinfeld demonstrated one way of giving telemarketers a better perspective on helping and hurting. Receiving yet another call at home around dinnertime, Seinfeld asked the telemarketer for his home phone number so Jerry could call him back at a later date around dinnertime. When the telemarketer refused, saying it would be an imposition, Jerry responded, "Well, now you know how I feel," and hung up. By the way, I don't advocate this approach as there are just too many telemarketers, and Jerry's behavior was rude for comedic effect. As an alternative, ask to be put on their do-not-call list, which many states require telemarketing firms to maintain by law.)

In many instances, we throw away the advantage of helping or hurting others, or it is negotiated away. It is not uncommon, for example, to have contractors ask for half or more of the payment for a job before starting, claiming that they need to purchase supplies, or to ask for full payment when the work is half completed. Do not be surprised if the work slows down once payment is received in full, as they attend to other jobs at other sites.

Many skilled negotiators are as adroit at convincing their counterparts that they can help them as they are at convincing the same parties or others that they can hurt them. Stephen Yokich, president of the United Automobile Workers (UAW), became a golfing partner and developed a close personal relationship with Ford Motor Company's Executive Vice President Peter Pestillo, which led to a relatively painless negotiation between the union and Ford management in 1996. But when talks with General Motors stalled later that year, Yokich orchestrated two local unions to call strikes at high-profit GM plants. With losses reaching a staggering $50 million a day, GM negotiators resumed 'round-the-clock negotiations, and an agreement quickly followed.

Many years ago, I worked as a mediator handling small-claims cases and civil disputes destined for court. As mediator, my job was to bring the disputing parties together, provide a structure for them to communicate, and help the parties work toward an agreement. I did not have the power, however, to dictate the outcome of the dispute (which an arbitrator or judge could do). I did a lot of negotiating to get the disputing parties together and keep them working on an agreement. Often things would break down at some point, and one of the parties would say something about walking out. Up to that point, my goal was to show competence, remain neutral, and provide a safe and constructive setting for interaction. This is how mediation might *help* them. But if things began to break down, I would ask the less-motivated party in private if he had ever been to court. Then I would matter-of-factly describe the court "alternative"— including the crowded courtroom setting, the delays and lengthy procedures once one gets to court (which translates into time lost from work), the potential attorney's fees, the uncertain consequences of a settlement. This is how not pursuing mediation can *hurt* the disputants. Generally, this subtle negotiation tactic was sufficient to refocus and reinvigorate one or both parties.

Sometimes the pressure points for helping or hurting the other party are structural, that is, built into the system. Lockheed Martin has been designing and testing an advanced tactical fighter for the U.S. Air Force, the F-22, for more than a decade. Although the F-22 has its share of critics, it survives because the parts are made in forty-three states. Forty-three states are *helped* economically, and forty-three states could be *hurt* through lost jobs and lost tax revenues if the project is scrapped. Each state has two senators and at least one congressperson in whose district a subcontractor is a major employer.

Recognizing how you can help or hurt the other party is part of the art of negotiation. Skilled negotiators instinctively know the needs of the other party. Salespeople can quickly read the body language of a consumer and tell if she is just browsing or a motivated buyer . . . and what is motivating her. They also are skilled in creating a sense of need on the part of a consumer, turning a browser into a buyer.

Let's try a simple scenario and see how adroit you are at identifying ways of helping and hurting your counterpart.

It's Sunday evening and you have invited a small group of

friends (six total) over for late afternoon socializing and evening dinner. As six o'clock approaches, you all begin to think about food. There is a service you can use that allows you to order from any one of fifty restaurants, each of which delivers for a 10 percent service charge. After some discussion, the group decides on an upscale Mexican restaurant that someone has enjoyed before; you call in your order. The restaurant claims to be out of one dish (salmon), but then they say they do have it. They're also out of certain appetizers that come with the entrees. Finally, the order is complete, with delivery expected in an hour and fifteen minutes.

An hour and a half later, the food has not yet arrived. Since one or two in your party need to head home soon, someone calls the restaurant. You are told that the food is on the way. People in the party are unhappy about the slow service. It has now been more than two hours. Someone calls again, and while he is on the phone the food arrives. Several in the group feel that the bill should be discounted for the slow service and missing appetizers.

How can you help the restaurant? How can you hurt the restaurant? List answers in the following boxes.

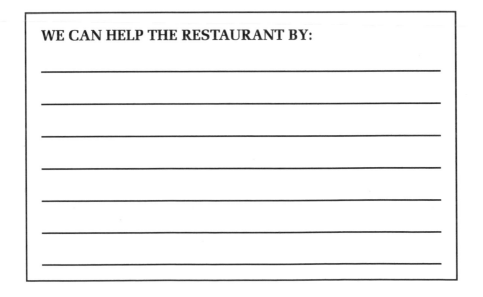

WE CAN HELP THE RESTAURANT BY:

WE CAN HURT THE RESTAURANT BY:

_____

_____

_____

_____

_____

_____

What are the ways that the restaurant can help or hurt you?

THE RESTAURANT CAN HELP US BY:

_____

_____

_____

_____

_____

_____

THE RESTAURANT CAN HURT US BY:

_____

_____

_____

_____

_____

_____

_____

Here are some ideas that might have occurred to you. Check the boxes corresponding to the ones you wrote down, and total the number of checks. Then, at the bottom of the checklist, add any additional ideas you had that I have not listed.

We can help the restaurant by:

- ☐ Paying our bill in full with a smile
- ☐ Continuing to use their service
- ☐ Recommending the food and service to others

We can hurt the restaurant by:

- ☐ Delaying payment of our bill (which keeps the delivery person from being on time to other locations and possibly upsets other customers)
- ☐ Refusing to accept the food
- ☐ Refusing to pay the bill (in total or in part)
- ☐ Keeping the party on the phone from attending to other matters
- ☐ Calling the Better Business Bureau

☐ Putting a stop-payment on our check

☐ Telling others about the restaurant's poor service

The restaurant can help us by:

☐ Offering a discount on our order

☐ Offering a discount on a future order

☐ Providing free appetizers or beverage

☐ Giving us a special table the next time we come into the restaurant

☐ Apologizing and promising this will never happen again

☐ Offering to cancel the order

The restaurant can hurt us by:

☐ Refusing to serve us again

☐ Reporting us to the organization of restaurants that provides this service (perhaps banning us from the service)

☐ Reporting us as a bad credit risk

_____ Number of boxes checked

Additional ideas of your own:

_____

_____

_____

_____

_____

_____

_____ Add number of ideas of your own

_____ Total number of ideas

A good score for this exercise is between 10 and 15, and anything greater than 15 is excellent. You might also want to examine, however, the categories in which most of your ideas occur. You might sometimes overestimate the power of the other party (that is, how he or she can help or hurt you) and underestimate your own power. How many ideas did you come up with for helping or hurting the restaurant? How many ideas did you have as to how the restaurant could help or hurt you?

Of course, thinking of ways you can help or hurt another party can be much more difficult if your blood is boiling, or you are shocked or emotionally wounded. Nonetheless, your ability to identify these pressure points can make all the difference in a negotiation.

3

Three Fundamental Questions of Negotiation

Improvisation is too good to leave to chance.
—Paul Simon

If only negotiating were as simple as memorizing and applying the Golden Rule of Chapter 2! Unfortunately, it's a bit more involved than this (although remembering the Golden Rule can take you a long way, both in negotiating and in completing your degree at the Five-Minute University).

There are three fundamental questions you need to ask yourself in preparation for a negotiation. The more important the negotiation, and the less skilled you are as a negotiator, the more essential it is to think through these questions carefully prior to engaging the other party.

What Do You Want?

The first question to ask yourself before a negotiation is, *What do I want?*

* Do you want to sell your house within three months?
* Do you want to lease with the option to buy?
* Do you want to hire this job applicant?
* Do you want to see the latest Harrison Ford movie?
* Do you want a new Corvette—in red?

As simple as this question might seem, it is not. There are several reasons for this. First, knowing what you want often involves more than one issue, concern, or item. Not only do I want to sell my house within three months, but I want to sell it for X. I want to see the latest Harrison Ford movie, and I want to go to the late show. I want to hire this job applicant—but I want him to start within the week, I want him to agree to a salary under $50K, and I want him to relocate to Houston.

Second, some of these issues are more important than others, yet there is a tendency to lump them all together or think of them as equally significant. Is it as important to hire this applicant as it is to have him start work within the week? Which is more important? It is worthwhile to think in terms of what you *must* have and what you would *like* to have . . . that is, to prioritize your wants and needs.

Third, you generally have some unspoken or subconscious issues or desires. It could be that these are things you take for granted (the new employee will pay his own relocation expenses), or issues that you are repressing for some reason (you are secretly in love with Harrison Ford and don't want your significant other to become jealous, be self-conscious, or think less of you). These subconscious issues may be just as powerful as your stated desires, but unless you are able to recognize or acknowledge them it is difficult to negotiate.

Finally, though you want to be clear in your own mind about what you want, nimbleness is one of the keys to successful face-to-face negotiations.

Let's suppose that you want to rent a one-bedroom beach house for a week, and that you want to spend no more than $1,500. You might be inclined to approach prospective lessors directly, with a clear statement of your desires—a one-bedroom house on the beach for one week for under $1,500. But doing so misses out on an opportunity to rent the house for less, or to rent a larger house for the same price. As the old saying goes, "Be careful what you ask for, because you just might get it." In other words, you need to be firm yet flexible about what you want, open to opportunities. And although you should think through what it is you want, it may be better not to blurt it out.

Because your answer to this first question can involve multiple reasons, you might want to take the time to put them down on paper. Recording and organizing your thoughts helps gain a better perspective. In negotiating, listing (and rating or ranking) what you want is particularly useful if the situation is complex or you are feeling pressured in some way. This becomes even more essential when "you" are a group or team rather than a single individual, in which case all of the issues highlighted previously are multiplied by the size of the group.

Why Should They Negotiate With You?

The second question you need to ask yourself before entering a negotiation is, *Why should the other party negotiate with me?* You might recognize that this question bears a close resemblance to our Golden Rule of negotiation, which states that people will not negotiate with you unless they believe you can help them or hurt them. How important is this negotiation to the other party? What options do they have? Is your smile so sweet that they will go along with your terms to gain your friendship or fondly recall the moment forever? Are you joined through work or family, which means you cannot easily get away from each other? Does winning this negotiation mean losing something else later on?

When you go into a retail store, more often than not you want to buy something. This is an automatic signal to the salesclerk that you have a problem or a need and that you believe this store might be able to solve the problem or satisfy the need. The salesclerk knows this implicitly—as do the mechanics in an auto repair shop, the people installing your new telephone line, and the scalpers selling tickets outside a stadium. They know why you are doing business with them. Why should they negotiate with you?

Believe it or not, in *every* situation there are ways that you can help the other party, as well as ways in which you can hurt him. Think about this for a moment. How can you help the mechanic to whom you are about to turn over your car? How can you help the phone installation person who expects you to be home, waiting, all day? How can you help the scalper whose tickets you want to buy?*

You might find it easier to answer this second question if you break down human needs into some basic categories. Think about how you can help or hurt the other party:

* Financially
* Psychologically
* Socially
* Materially
* Physically

When you ask your waitperson to make you a special dish— something not listed on the menu—why should she accommodate you? Is it because you come to the restaurant frequently and the kitchen is not busy right now? because you have just moved into the neighborhood and could become a regular customer? because you are friendly, sociable, amusing? because the special dish is relatively easy to make? because she would expect a larger tip?

Many times, one of these needs or worries is more pressing than the others, and often there is more than one way to satisfy the need. In addition, needs can change over time. For example, when you arrive early at a moving sale or an estate sale, the sellers are likely to decline offers below the listed price; they are trying to get as much value for each item as possible (financial needs). However, near the end of the day their needs change as the thought of having to box and lug the unsold items becomes dreadfully apparent, not to mention potential storage costs (financial, material, and physical needs).

If you don't know what the other party's needs are, you have to discover them. More on discovering the problems and needs of the other party later.

---

*Here are some ideas: Find out if the mechanic likes sports, discuss local teams, and mention that you might have an extra ticket to a game. Find out what desserts the installer craves and make sure he or she knows you will have some waiting early in the morning. Point out that a lot of people seem to be selling tickets, mention that security police are everywhere, ask if he or she will have extra tickets in the future.

What Are Your Alternatives?

The third question you should ask yourself has already been hinted at: *What are my alternatives?* That is, what options do you have if this negotiation fails? What do you do if you or the other party walks away from an agreement?

Roger Fisher and William Ury, in their now-classic book *Getting to Yes* (1991), talk about having a Best Alternative to a Negotiated Agreement (BATNA). If, going into a negotiation, you have an alternative to reaching an agreement, then you negotiate more comfortably knowing that you can always walk. The more important this negotiation is to you, the more essential it is to have an alternative that is equally as attractive as a negotiated agreement. If it is not a real alternative, you are not likely to be able to fool yourself or the other party. (There are exceptions to this characterization of the average negotiator; some people seem not to care about even the most crucial negotiations. But they are in the distinct minority.)

To illustrate, there was a time when a colleague of mine was interested in a position as a visiting professor at an East Coast university. Ultimately, she wanted to leave the university where she was working and the small city where she was living, and perhaps teach in a department that came closer to her academic training. When she went for the interview, the chair of the department let it be known that the other two prospective visiting professors would not be coming after all (in fact, one had just telephoned his decision), so they were really counting on my colleague to fill a slot. This was useful information because it told her how she could help them or hurt them.

But this candidate had something else going for her. She had been offered an opportunity through her current university to travel to England for a semester and teach North American students in a castle. She had traveled to Europe some fifteen years earlier and had many fond memories. Returning would be nice, and the opportunity would take her to a metropolitan environment (albeit temporarily), which is what she wanted. Consequently, she was very relaxed in her negotiations and able to negotiate from a position of power because she had an alternative to a negotiated agreement with the East Coast university. At one point, she shared this alternative with the chair of the department; later, when they appeared to be at an impasse on an issue, she said that if they could not work out an arrangement, it was OK; she would go with the European alternative.

She not only got the appointment but received a higher salary than was initially offered, with a reduced teaching load and the promise that she could teach a special course. They also paid her moving expenses, which at that time was unusual for a visiting appointment. She owed a good part of this to having a Best Alternative to a Negotiated Agreement.

BATNA is an important concept because it relates not only to you but also to the other party. The answer to your prior question—*Why should the other party negotiate with me?*—is determined by this party's needs and options. The more options the other party has, the more flexibility he or she has to satisfy those needs, regardless of how severe they might be. In other words, if the other party has a BATNA (or several BATNAs), he or she might not be as motivated to negotiate with you.

Charles Schulz, the creator of the comic strip Peanuts, tells the story of the time he was approached by a television network about a possible Saturday morning cartoon series based on Charlie Brown's lovable dog, Snoopy. At the time, Peanuts was a very popular, syndicated comic strip. Schulz wrote eight episodes for the new series and sent them to an animator, who in turn sent the cartoons on to the network producers. A couple of weeks went by and Schulz heard nothing. He couldn't understand it. Finally, they rejected the idea because Snoopy and his brothers and sisters could not talk. To Charles Schulz's amazement, the producers never even called to discuss their concerns! So what if Schulz was miffed. In New York and Hollywood, there is a never-ending surplus of ideas and talent, so producers have many, many BATNAs.

Table 3-1 lists some of the potential consequences of failing to ask yourself these three fundamental questions of negotiation. You may recognize these consequences from one or more of your prior negotiations. The process and, ultimately, the outcome of a negotiation can suffer.

Table 3-1: What Happens If You Fail to Ask Yourself the Three Fundamental Questions:

Not asking yourself:	Can lead to:
What do I want?	Confusion
	Loss of control or respect
	Settling for a package rather than a priority outcome (partial-win outcome)
Why should the other party negotiate with me?	Being ignored by the other party
	Fewer concessions by the other party
	Increased likelihood of partial-win outcome
What is my BATNA?	Reduced confidence
	Less willingness to pursue sensitive or explosive issues*
	Increased likelihood of partial-win outcome

Your Next Negotiation

It is time to put these three questions to use. I indicated in the Introduction to the book that you would have the opportunity to practice some negotiations with your spouse, friends, coworkers, or others, to measure your progress. The first of these, a simple ten-minute negotiation, is in the next chapter.

Have you secured a negotiating partner/opponent? Securing a negotiation partner is itself a negotiation, not that different from asking a neighbor if you can borrow a tool, "inviting" a friend to help paint rooms at your son's or daughter's school, asking someone to give your dead car battery a jump, or requesting assistance on a project at work.

If you haven't found a negotiating partner yet, this is your first negotiation. Let's apply the three fundamental questions to your situation. What do you want? Think about it carefully and write your response to this initial question in the box below.

WHAT DO I WANT?

_____

_____

_____

_____

_____

You may be inclined to give a simple, straightforward response to this question, something like "To get someone to negotiate with me." In fact, you want someone to negotiate with you for ten minutes. This is important information to keep in mind in approaching a potential negotiator: It's only ten minutes. Also, you may want the other party to participate willingly and with enthusiasm. You want the experience itself to be a reward, so that you are not expected to pay back the favor later.

Now, the second question:

WHY SHOULD THE OTHER PARTY NEGOTIATE WITH ME?

_____

_____

_____

_____

_____

The answer to this question might be because the other party is bored, can easily spare ten minutes, owes you a favor, likes interpersonal games, wants to learn something about negotiation, etc. Think about the other party's needs. How can you help him or her?

Finally,

WHAT ARE MY ALTERNATIVES?

_____

_____

_____

_____

_____

Who else might negotiate with you if this person cannot or will not negotiate?

Using this information, negotiate to obtain a partner for the extended exercise in Chapter 4. While you are reading the first few pages of the next chapter, you might want to ask your negotiating partner to pull a couple of oranges from the refrigerator to serve as props. (If you don't have any oranges, you can substitute two lemons or limes—or imaginary oranges.)

4

The Art of Discovery

A wise man will make more opportunities than he finds.

—Francis Bacon

There is a well-known maxim in the real estate profession that the three most important elements when buying property are location, location, and location. A similar statement applies to the art and science of negotiation. If you think about the Golden Rule of negotiation, the three fundamental questions of negotiation, and the negotiation with the department chair described in Chapter 3, you might recognize that the three most important elements of negotiation are information, information, and information. The more information you have about yourself and your needs (fundamental question number one), the other party's needs (fundamental question number two), and your alternatives (fundamental question number three), the better off you are.

In the first chapter of this book, I defined negotiation in relatively broad terms and distinguished it from bargaining. More than just haggling or bartering over two monetary positions, negotiation can involve discovery of respective needs and mutual interests, resulting in a breakthrough that leaves a smile on everyone's face. The outcome of such a discovery or breakthrough is sometimes referred to as a win-win solution or outcome. Simply put, a win-win negotiation is one in which both parties feel that they have gotten what they want. (If three parties are involved, this would be win-win-win, or "win cubed.") Win-win negotiations contrast with

1. Win-lose negotiations, in which one person wins and the other person loses
2. Lose-lose negotiations, where both parties feel they have lost (most divorce proceedings involving lawyers are lose-lose—or lose-lose-win-win, if you include the two lawyers)
3. Partial-win, partial-lose outcomes, where the parties feel they got some of what they wanted but not everything that was important

In reality, outcomes to a negotiation are not so easily categorized as one of the four types, but you get the idea.

The Elusive Win-Win Negotiation

There was a time when finding those win-win outcomes was highly touted by management gurus and self-help authors. The truth is, they are difficult to find. Because they are exceptional, we often assume that it is not possible to effect a win-win outcome, and so we settle for some form of compromise (a partial-win, partial-lose). Unfortunately, this becomes a self-fulfilling prophecy.

The key to finding win-win outcomes is information. The more information you have about your resources, your needs, the other party's needs or desires, and his resources, the greater the likelihood of discovering a breakthrough, win-win outcome. Sometimes you have this information in advance of a negotiation, but just as often you must mutually explore individual needs and resources to discover the hidden solution.

As an illustration, consider the roles for a simple two-person negotiation described in the following pages. The negotiation involves oranges. You should read "Your role," and ask your husband, wife, colleague, or friend to read "Other role" and play the second part. (No fair peeking at the other role.) See if the two of you can come up with an agreement in five or ten minutes.

YOUR ROLE:

It is a very warm, humid day, and you have just come home from exercising. All the way home you were thinking about the juicy oranges you bought yesterday, chilling in the refrigerator, and how thirsty you are.

As you enter the house, you discover that your housemate is in the kitchen making something. It is even warmer in the kitchen, because the oven is on. You extend a quick hello and move toward the refrigerator. But before you get there, your housemate opens the refrigerator door, pulls out the last two oranges, and puts them on the counter next to some flour and a mixing bowl.

Your immediate response is: "Hey, I was going to eat those!"

OTHER ROLE:

You are making a cake for the house party this evening. Since the theme of the party is "The Tropics," you have decided to make an orange-flavored cake. There are a lot of things to do before the party, and the cake needs to cool before you can frost it. The oven is warming up and everything is mixed except for the orange flavoring that needs to be added. You remember that there were four oranges in the refrigerator, and you're turning to get them when one of your housemates returns. You discover that there are only two oranges left, but that should be enough. As you remove them from the refrigerator, your housemate declares: "Hey, I was going to eat those!"

Evaluating Your Negotiation

What kind of resolution or agreement did you come up with? Record your agreement in the following box:

I have seen a lot of dyads tackle this problem, where each side is given a role to play. And I have seen a lot of win-lose or partial-win, partial-lose solutions: invoking buyer's rights, dividing the oranges (each getting one, or one-and-a-half and one-half), stealing the oranges, offering cake for orange juice, offering an invitation to the party for the oranges, getting the housemate to substitute another citrus flavor, jogging down to the market for more oranges, driving down to the market, and no resolution (stalemate).

One of the keys to discovering breakthrough outcomes is recognizing the difference between *positions* and *interests*, and finding a way to move from the former to the latter. Many negotiation deadlocks occur even before a face-to-face encounter, as we anticipate how we think the other party will react and we concoct logic to argue our position. In this simple scenario with the oranges, each side can very quickly settle into identical positions: I need the oranges. All of the energy is then devoted to defending these positions.

The key to a win-win outcome in this case, as in many situations, is to move away from positions by discovering the true interests of one or both parties (see figure). Interests are the broader goals served by a party's position. Discovering one's interests usually involves asking some variation of the question "Why?" *Why do you want these two oranges?* For one individual, the answer is because he or she is thirsty (and perhaps wants something cold and nutritious to drink). For the other individual, the answer might be to give a citrus flavor to the cake. (This latter response begs for another round of "Why?" *Why citrus flavor?*) One creative solution to the conflict is to peel the oranges. You get the pulp and juice to quench your thirst, cool down, and restore nutrients; your housemate can use shavings from the peel to give a citrus flavor to the cake. Both parties get exactly what they want; it's a win-win outcome.

INTERESTS	To quench thirst, to cool down, to restore nutrients	To flavor cake for "The Tropics" party
	^	^
	|	|
	|	|
	|	|
	|	|
	| Why?	| Why?
	|	|
	|	|
	|	|
	|	|
	|	|
POSITIONS	I "need" the oranges	I "need" the oranges

Unless one of you knows that shavings from the peel of a citrus fruit can give flavor to a pie or cake, this solution may elude you. But in any negotiation, information is often a critical ingredient. The more you know about your own needs, the other party's needs, and the properties of the issues or items with which you are working (oranges, automobiles, movies currently playing, work schedules, salaries), the more effective you can be as a negotiator.

Note that in the figure illustrating the concept of positions versus interests I put the word *need* in quotation marks. Frequently, you translate your "wants" into "needs" as you contemplate engaging in a potentially difficult negotiation. You recognize, perhaps subconsciously, that the other party is likely to give more credence to your demands if they involve needs (that is, necessities) rather than wants (your desires). So don't be distracted or discouraged if your counterpart says "I *need* those," since more often than not she is declaring a position rather than an interest.

Here is a further illustration of the positions-to-interests transformation. Your neighbor of four years is thinking of putting a fence atop the retaining wall that joins your two properties. It is not a case of good fences making good neighbors, since you have always gotten along with all your neighbors, including— and especially—the Wagner family next door. However, the Wagners have two children, ages two and three, who sometimes play in the backyard. They are concerned about the children falling off the retaining wall, which reaches a height of almost six feet at its tallest point. You are concerned that a fence will block the sunlight to plants in that corner of your property and destroy the view you have from your backyard patio.

It would be easy for you and the Wagners to get locked into your positions—to fence or not to fence—and lose sight of your respective interests. You want natural sunlight for your plants and an unimpeded view; the Wagners want to ensure the safety of their children. They may also want to maintain a sense of spatial openness while installing something that is attractive and low maintenance. A wrought-iron fence of moderate height (3 to $3\frac{1}{2}$ feet) could satisfy your interests as well as those of the Wagners. But you need to know a bit about different types of fences. Most importantly, you have to move past positions to discover your individual and mutual interests.

This reformulation process is important in all types of negotiations, even international ones. In the 1990s, many industrialized nations began to voice concerns about the world's dwindling tropical forests. These forests help provide the clean air and water essential to life and are habitats for many of the planet's rare and endangered species. Less-developed countries, within whose borders most of these forests reside, countered that the industrialized nations have no right to dictate how their tropical forests are used since most industrialized nations built their economies at the expense of their own forests, and the heavy industries of these same nations are responsible for much of the world's pollution. Thus, each side seemed steadfast in its position regarding whether or not to harvest the forests.

Beyond these positions, however, were mutual interests in maintaining a healthy environment and biodiversity. In addition, the interests of less-developed countries included extracting some value from their natural resources to promote economic development. Although a variety of technical devices (including satellites) are now being employed to monitor and protect these forests, less-developed countries are benefiting economically through a host of joint ventures. These include ecotourism, bioprospecting agreements (in which pharmaceutical firms pay for the right to extract chemicals from plants, animals, and microbes), and emissions exchanges (by which a power company from a developed country, to compensate for carbon dioxide emissions, purchases several thousand acres of forest in a less-developed country as a natural preserve to offset the release of carbon dioxide).

Oddly enough, sometimes having more than one issue, or creating additional issues, can help you negotiate win-win outcomes. With a single issue, there is a tendency to treat things as your way or my way, win or lose, go or no-go. A management-labor dispute over wages looks like a fixed-pie negotiation: The more one side gets, the less the other side gets. If a situation is viewed as a single issue, the tendency is to bargain rather than to negotiate in the broad sense. But if there are a whole set of issues, it may be possible to give both sides much of what they want because in all likelihood some issues are more important to one party whereas other issues are more significant to the other party. (Remember our discussion of the multiplicity of wants or needs in answer to the first fundamental question, *What do I want?*) In the case of a management-labor dispute, a host of other issues can be brought into play: profit-sharing plans, sick leave, overtime, strike policies, outsourcing practices, downsizing, automation, and work breaks.

Reprinted with special permission of King Features Syndicate.

In general, the more that the issues at stake can be divided into items that are valued more by one party than they cost the other party, the greater the chances of a successful outcome. In terms of the contested oranges, the peel is valuable to the party baking the cake but is little to lose for the thirsty party, while the value and cost of the pulp is just the opposite. David Lax and James Sebenius (1986) refer to people who are able to identify these opportunities as *value creators*. Their opposites are *value claimers*, people who simply want a larger slice of the fixed pie (or oranges, in this case). Sometimes, though, even when the obvious is looking you straight in the face, it is difficult to recognize these opportunities without some assistance (as the Sam & Silo cartoon aptly illustrates). If you can never see these opportunities, it may be due to your negotiating style. But more on negotiation styles later. Let's look next at some of the behaviors of effective negotiators.

5

Behaviors of Successful Negotiators

The ideal attitude is to be physically loose and mentally tight.

—Arthur Ashe

You would think (hope) that someone might do a study of negotiators to determine what separates the more successful from those who struggle with negotiating. One such study was carried out by Neil Rackham (1999), with forty-eight labor relations negotiators who frequently act as third-party negotiators. In this study, the negotiators were deemed successful (or skilled) based on three criteria:

1. They had a track record of significant success.
2. They were rated as effective by both parties to a negotiation.
3. They had a low incidence of implementation failures (that is, the agreements they negotiated were implemented and endured).

These forty-eight negotiators were studied over a total of 102 negotiating sessions, and their behaviors were compared with those of a group of average negotiators. Here is what Rackham found for eight behaviors employed in face-to-face encounters: four behaviors that skilled negotiators used more frequently than the average negotiators, and four behaviors that the skilled negotiators used less frequently.

Four Desirable Behaviors

Asking Questions

Recalling my earlier claim that the three most important elements of negotiation are information, information, and information, you should not be surprised to learn that Rackham found the skilled negotiators were more than twice as likely to ask questions than were the average negotiators. These included open-ended questions ("How has business been lately?" "How can I help you?" "What are you hoping to get out of this negotiation?" "Why do you want the oranges?") as well as close-ended questions (which can be answered yes or no, or with a single word or phrase).

Here are the reasons most frequently given for this behavior by the skilled negotiators:

* To gather data about the other party's thinking or position
* To control the discussion
* To keep the other party active, reduce his or her thinking time
* To give you thinking time (while the other party responds)
* To avoid direct disagreements

Open-ended questions are particularly useful at the beginning of a negotiation, since they yield a great deal of information about what is foremost on the other party's mind as well as suggest an interest in the other party's needs, a willingness to listen, and an openness. Open-ended questions later in a negotiation can shift the focus back to the other party if discussions become delicate or emotional, or if you reach an impasse. For example, your neighbor wants to put up a wooden fence because wood is inexpensive; but a wooden fence will clearly obstruct sunlight and your view, so you ask: "How well do you think it will hold up?"

Testing Understanding and Summarizing

In Rackham's study, compared to the average negotiators the skilled negotiators were more than twice as likely to test the

37

other party's understanding of a prior statement, and nearly twice as likely to summarize the previous points in a discussion. Testing understanding can be accomplished in a variety of ways, including an interpretive approach ("So, you want the product shipped by Friday not only to meet the terms of the agreement but also to free up inventory space") or the Rogerian (from Carl Rogers) approach of simply repeating what the other party has just said in the form of a question (the other party says, "We can't afford to have this new product shipped late," to which you reply, "You can't afford to have the new product shipped late?"). The Rogerian form of questioning is an implicit "Why?" that often reveals the interests behind someone's position. Summarizing is simply putting in your own words what has been discussed and decided so far; as an example, "If I can summarize, it sounds like we are in agreement on three points: 1. we both want. . . ."

Both of these behaviors—testing understanding and summarizing—involve making discussion points clearer and more specific. Rackham found that the average negotiator was often so concerned that the other party would not come to an agreement if certain points were included in the final package that he would allow issues and expectations to remain fuzzy to avoid that outcome. This almost certainly ensures problems later on.

Inexperienced management consultants, for example, sometimes hedge in attempting to negotiate psychological and literal contracts with a client. If a consultant is asked to assist an organization in dealing with one or more problems, the individual contacting and hiring the consultant more often than not has a specific idea of what the problem is, how it should be solved, how quickly the problem should be dispatched, and what it will cost. But in fact the presenting problem may only be a symptom of the real problem, which is more difficult to identify and deal with. Wanting the contract, an unskilled consultant hedges on services and cost. But when the client eventually discovers that this is taking longer, costing more, and not addressing what was originally "agreed to," both the psychological and literal contracts are threatened. In contrast, a skilled and confident consultant clarifies expectations up front, being true to her goals and values as well as the client's desires, while continuing to reinforce (or renegotiate, if necessary) mutual expectations.*

Giving Internal Information

Giving internal information is an interesting behavior, perhaps one that you might not expect to find among skilled negotiators. It is certainly a behavior that I have found difficult to cultivate, but it puts me in good stead if and when I am able to use it.

If another party presents an argument or makes a proposal, you may have mixed feelings about it. You may not trust the information, or you can see both advantages and disadvantages to the proposal. Without giving information about your position (facts, sources, options, etc.), you can be straightforward and honest in expressing your feelings about what the other party has said. You can also express your feelings matter-of-factly, and mostly unemotionally (that is, without anger, frustration, disappointment, suspicion, or sanctimony), since an emotional response can signal that this negotiation is important to you and thus give the other party an advantage.

For example, your supervisor comes to you with a request to work this weekend. The company needs to get out a response to a request-for-proposal (RFP), which must be postmarked Monday at the latest. You have other plans for the weekend, but you know the importance of putting in a successful bid. You might respond by describing just those mixed feelings: "What I hear you saying is that it's important to respond to this RFP, and to mail in our bid by Monday. I would like to work on the proposal, but it may be difficult for me to work this weekend. Can you tell me more about what needs to be done on the proposal?" Such a response is likely to elicit additional information from your supervisor, information that might help one or both of you identify a win-win outcome. Once again, Rackham found that the skilled negotiators were nearly twice as likely as the average negotiators were to use this behavior.

*Early in my training I was taught the "principle of no surprises": No client wants to be surprised or embarrassed, so there needs to be continuous dialogue concerning goals and processes.

Explaining Before Disagreeing

If you are like me, you have a tendency to state your final conclusion before going into an explanation of how you arrived at the result. In a dispute or a negotiation, doing so might come out like this: "No, I disagree. Let me tell you why. The Model X-19 is not as durable, contains fewer features, and is costly to repair." Or, in the case of the contested oranges: "No, the oranges are mine! I'm dehydrated and need some juice."

Even if your reasoning is sound, by first stating your conclusion (disagreement) you touch off an emotional reaction from the other party. It is not the response the other party is expecting. Nor is it the response he wants to hear. Consequently, there is a good chance that it is difficult for him to hear your explanation, either because of the stunning effect of your conclusion or because the other party has begun to construct a counterargument.

According to Rackham, skilled negotiators are more likely to begin with a review of events or circumstances—an explanation of reasoning—leading up to a statement of disagreement. (You might even begin with behavioral labeling: "Can I tell you what I am thinking?") In this way, it is possible for the other party to hear your arguments, follow your logic, and perhaps arrive at the same conclusion that you have.*

Four Undesirable Behaviors

In his research, Neil Rackham also found some behaviors that skilled negotiators used less frequently than did average negotiators.

Defend-and-Attack

It is easy to get caught up in the emotion of a negotiation, one that is turning sour, and resort to tit-for-tat behaviors that produce an

*Developing this skill may be more challenging for introverts than extraverts. Introverts are more likely to *think* through the logic of a position or conclusion before announcing their decision, rather than talk through it. Instead of trying to change this "internal processing" characteristic, an introvert might practice verbally reconstructing the logic before sharing her decision.

escalating exchange of charges and countercharges. One way this happens is if a comment or claim is made that you feel is incorrect, unwarranted, or unfair. It may be that the charge is made in the presence of associates, clients, or the press, and you feel of necessity that you must defend your honor to save face. If the charge is true, you claim that others are guilty of the same behavior (including your counterpart).

Rackham found that the average negotiators were more than three times as likely as the skilled negotiators to engage in a defend-and-attack spiral. That is, if attacked, the average negotiators' reaction was more often to defend prior behavior (and positions) and to put the charging opponent on the defensive by counterattacking. Indeed, this was almost a gradual process, with things slowly getting out of hand.

One course of action, which might seem difficult to do at first, is to acknowledge your behavior and apologize. If you can bring yourself to do this honestly and nondefensively, you will in all likelihood see an immediate change in the mood of the other party. The anger and emotion will drain from his body, from head to toe, and you can move on to a discussion of future behavior.

A second approach is to ask an open-ended question ("Why do you feel this way?" "What would you like to see happen?" "What can I do to help?") or redirect the discussion to common goals ("Okay, before we get caught up in a battle of words . . . we both want to see this proposal get completed on time and funded."). In some cases, this amounts to an implicit acknowledgment of responsibility. However, if the other party feels aggrieved, you may not be able to move forward without acknowledgment or apology.

Finally, if the issues are very important or very sensitive, it may be easier for a third party or other agent to handle this than for the principal protagonists to try to resolve things themselves. This is one reason why most divorcing couples hire lawyers.

Argument Dilution

You might expect that the way to win a debate is to provide more arguments than your opponent. If I can think of two reasons for doing something and you can think of five reasons for not doing it, you win the argument. In the contested-oranges negotiation, your housemate argues that she saw the oranges first and the party is tonight. You counter that you checked the oranges before you headed out for a jog; you bought the oranges; you have hardly eaten any of them; and you are hot, dehydrated, and need to replace lost nutrients.

Surprisingly, when it comes to offering arguments to support a particular point of view or course of action in negotiating, Rackham found skilled negotiators were more likely to offer one or two strong arguments rather than one strong argument and several minor arguments, or a string of relatively minor arguments. The latter approaches were more common among the average negotiators. Offering incidental supporting arguments tended to dilute the strength of a main argument. Instead, the skilled negotiators would continue to pound home the primary argument, only switching to the other arguments if they were clearly losing ground in the bargaining phase of the negotiation.

Political candidates are well aware of argument dilution in their negotiations with voters. When they find a single issue that resonates with the public—an argument or challenge that their opponents don't have an answer for ("Are you better off today than you were four years ago?")—they keep playing it. If you are trying to get your city's public works department to repair the alley in back of your building, you are better off consistently reminding it that fuel oil trucks are having a hard time getting back to many of the buildings, which could result in no heat for some families (and harm to children and the elderly of those families during the dead of winter) than to argue that first the condition of the alley is unsightly, second the garbage cans fall over because the pavement is uneven, third the suspension systems of cars using the alley could be damaged, and so forth.

Counterproposals

In terms of immediate counterproposals, Rackham found that the average negotiators offered them nearly twice as frequently as did the skilled negotiators. A counterproposal, in the form of a new issue (say, a product delivery date, in the case of a pricing proposal), additional option (another product), or completely different proposal (joint venture), complicates the negotiation, occurs when the other party is least receptive, and often appears as a blocking action. You find yourself falling into this behavior in the contested-oranges negotiation if you suggest that your "housemate" substitute another citrus flavor (lemon, lime) or forgo the citrus flavor altogether.

Offering an immediate counterproposal is a form of fighting positions with positions. You counter the other party's position with your own position. It suggests that you are more focused on your own self-interest than on acknowledging and understanding the other party's concerns or interests.

Rather than offering an immediate reaction, positive or negative, or offering a counterproposal, you might ask an open-ended question or request additional information: "Tell me more about this idea"; "Tell me again why you need the oranges." This helps you and your counterpart avoid digging deeper into your respective positions, and it creates a better climate for exploring the reasons behind the positions—namely, the interests.

Irritators

Finally, one of the temptations during negotiation is to let the other party know what a good deal she is getting. For example, during the latter stages of contracting, the party making the offer says, "I think you will find this to be *very fair*" (or "reasonable," or "most generous," or "more than fair").

This type of value judgment, aimed at suggesting to the other party that you are doing her a big favor and that she had better take the offer before you come to your senses, is called an *irritator* (gentle as it may seem). Irritators suggest implicitly that if I don't take your kind offer, then I am being unfair, unreasonable, or selfish. No one likes to be put into this predicament. In the negotiations that Rackham studied, the average negotiators were nearly five times as likely as were the skilled negotiators to use such irritators.

As an alternative, consider thinking (and commenting) in terms of joint progress and outcomes. For example, at the conclusion of a business negotiation, you are probably better off commenting on how much has been accomplished, reviewing the terms of your agreement, and indicating that you are looking forward to working with the other party (if there are future considerations).

Self-Analysis

These eight behaviors—four desirable and four undesirable—can play an important role in almost any type of negotiation. How would you rate yourself on using each of these eight behaviors? Think about the oranges negotiation. Think about other negotiations that you have had recently with your coworkers, supervisor, spouse, children, salespeople, mechanics, etc. Place an *X* on the following scales to indicate the extent to which you generally engage in each behavior.

Desirable Behaviors	*Use*		
Ask questions	Very infrequent	Moderately frequent	Very frequent
Test understanding or summarize discussions	Very infrequent	Moderately frequent	Very frequent
Share internal motives or feelings	Very infrequent	Moderately frequent	Very frequent
Explain your reasoning before disagreeing	Very infrequent	Moderately frequent	Very frequent
Undesirable Behaviors			
Defend your position(s) and counterattack	Very infrequent	Moderately frequent	Very frequent

Offer multiple, diluted arguments	Very infrequent	Moderately frequent	Very frequent
Make counterproposals	Very infrequent	Moderately frequent	Very frequent
Employ value statements (irritators)	Very infrequent	Moderately frequent	Very frequent

We all, of course, use these behaviors at various times. Depending upon the situation, it may make sense to offer counterproposals or multiple, diluted arguments. Raised to the level of a style, though, you will find that repeated and consistent use of counterproposals is less effective than some other behaviors (asking questions, testing understanding and summarizing discussion, etc.).

So, how do you rate yourself on these negotiation behaviors? Are there one or two specific behaviors that you use very infrequently when you should be using them much more frequently, or vice versa? You might want to check with a spouse or close friend to validate your assessment. Then, pick a behavior that you would like to change or acquire, record it, and commit yourself to using it sometime within the next twenty-four hours. It could be in a workplace negotiation, or a negotiation with your significant other concerning dinner and the movies. The more you practice this behavior, the more natural it becomes for you.

Behavior to change or acquire:

_____

If you believe yourself to be particularly resistant to acquiring this behavior, you might want to consider going overboard with your initial application. That is, exaggerate use (or nonuse) of the behavior to get a feel for what it is like to move to the other extreme. For example, if the behavior you need to develop is to ask questions, then go to a retail store where there are few customers and commence asking questions—about the store, the salesperson, the industry, competitors, the neighborhood, the weather, and of course the product. Give yourself a time frame (say, at least three minutes of questions). See how it feels. Then, in subsequent practice rounds, back off gradually from this extreme behavior until you find a comfortable yet effective pattern of questioning.

6

Measuring Your Progress

The Valero Wine–Continental Glass Negotiation

Even if you're on the right track, you'll get run over if you just sit there.

—Will Rogers

Let's see what you have incorporated thus far into your repertoire of negotiation behaviors. Once again, ask your husband or wife, a colleague, or a friend to assist you in this exercise by taking on one of the two roles. This negotiation is a bit more complicated than the conflict involving the oranges (in Chapter 4) and represents a buyer-seller business negotiation. You probably should allot fifteen to twenty minutes for actual face-to-face negotiating. Each negotiator has a set of confidential information. Do not read the other party's confidential background information, and think carefully before giving any of your confidential information to your counterpart.

The negotiation involves Valero Wine Company's purchasing a quantity of wine bottles from a bottle manufacturer, Continental Glass. You represent Valero Wine. Your background information follows, along with an agreement form to record the terms of your agreement. (You may want to use a calculator for this negotiation.) The background information for the negotiator representing Continental Glass can be found in Appendix A.

VALERO WINE COMPANY
(Confidential Facts)

Your organization, the Valero Wine Company, is a medium-sized company that has been in the wine business for more than sixty years. The company grows its own grapes and makes all varieties of wine, specializing in Chardonnay. Valero Wine has several large wine distilleries as well as a bottling, labeling, and packaging operation.

With the upcoming holiday season, Valero Wine is looking to capture a good slice of the market with an advertising blitz and a distinctive, gift-sized 100-ml bottle. (The normal size is 750 ml.) The ad campaign has been months in the making, and the first promotions will run in just over three weeks.

Unfortunately, the company that was to have supplied the gift-sized bottles, Cactus Glass, is having labor problems. It is likely that a strike will at least slow, if not halt, production at Cactus, a longtime supplier of bottles. This is an unusual size for a wine bottle, and production could take as much as two weeks or longer. You need 80,000 of the gift-sized 100-ml bottles within two weeks to meet your distribution schedule.

Continental Glass is another company that might be able to help you. It is a small operation but has been known to manufacture a variety of bottle sizes. As a representative of Valero Wine, you have been asked to determine whether Continental can meet your production needs and to negotiate a deal. Here are some facts that might help you:

1. Continental Glass is a relatively new company, probably looking to build long-term business relationships.
2. You would have paid Cactus Glass 15 cents per bottle.
3. To make a profit, you need to keep your costs below 20 cents per bottle.

Time is of the essence. You need 80,000 of the gift-sized bottles delivered within two weeks, and preferably in ten days. You are authorized to pay as much as 30 cents per bottle to get them on time. Record your agreement with the Continental Glass representative on the form that follows, signed by both representatives.

AGREEMENT FORM

Valero Wine Company agrees to purchase _____ 100-ml bottles from Continental Glass, to be delivered within _____ days of this agreement. The purchase price is _____.

Other conditions of this purchase are as follows:

_____

_____

_____

_____

_____

_____

_____

_____

_____

_____

_____

_____

_____	_____
(Valero Wine Representative)	(Continental Glass Representative)

Before you begin negotiating, let's go back to the three fundamental questions of negotiation, presented in Chapter 3, and attempt to answer each question.

Recall the first question (*What do I want?*). What outcome(s) would make this a successful negotiation for you? List your objectives in the box below.

WHAT DO I WANT?

_____

_____

_____

_____

Second, why should the other party negotiate with you? You know why you are negotiating. You know what you want. What does the other party want? Remember our Golden Rule of negotiating: People will not negotiate with you unless they believe you can help them or hurt them. How can you help the other party? Record your ideas in the box below.

WHY SHOULD THE OTHER PARTY NEGOTIATE WITH ME?

_____

_____

_____

_____

_____

You may have been hard pressed to list many ideas in this box. This is where several of the behaviors of successful negotiators described previously—most particularly asking questions and testing understanding or summarizing discussions—are important in learning about the other party's needs. (Hint: The representative from Continental Glass has needs; see if you can discover them in your negotiation.)

Finally, what are your alternatives? That is, what happens if you do not get a negotiated agreement? Do you have a fall-back strategy? Do you have a best alternative to a negotiated agreement? The stronger and more appealing your BATNA, the more effectively you can negotiate. Think about this carefully, and record your alternative(s) in the next box.

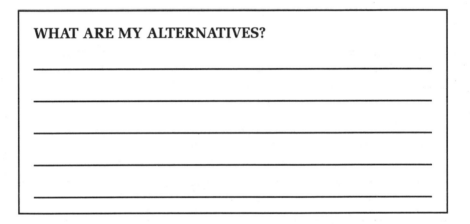

WHAT ARE MY ALTERNATIVES?

OK, let the negotiation begin. The confidential information for the representative from Continental Glass is in Appendix A. Once you have an agreement, record it on the Agreement Form, which each of you should sign.

Evaluating the Negotiation

Do you have a signed contract? If you do, exchange confidential information with the other representative (if you haven't done this already) so you can learn about each other's negotiating situation.

There are many ways to evaluate this negotiation. One, of course, is in terms of the number of bottles purchased and the price per bottle. As you can see from the following information, Continental Glass was willing to go as low as 5 cents (the recycling or scrap value) but would prefer a price between 10 and 15 cents, whereas Valero Wine would prefer between 15 and 20 cents but authorized you to spend as much as 30 cents per bottle. The typical settlement range for this exercise is 15–20 cents per bottle.

You might also look at this negotiation in terms of the number of bottles bought/sold, the delivery date, and any additional conditions to the agreement (such as shipping charges). Put an *X* on the scale in the figure below corresponding to your price per bottle.

```
                            Cents per bottle
| --------------[ --------------| --------------( ------------- ) --------------| --------------] ------------- | ------------- |
0            5            10           15          20           25           30          35           40

        Scrap value                  Typical                  Authorized
        (Continental)               settlement                  limit
                                      range                    (Valero)
```

Your final settlement largely depends on what you learned about the other party's needs and what he or she learned about your situation. (Remember the three most important elements of a negotiation: information, information, and information.) At the time of the agreement, were you able to learn that:

(Yes or no)

_____ 1. Continental Glass has done business with a distributor to the airlines?

_____ 2. The distributor had declared bankruptcy?

_____ 3. Continental Glass had 120,000 of the 100-ml bottles in stock?

_____ 4. The cost to Continental Glass of manufacturing this bottle is 10 cents per bottle?

_____ 5. Continental Glass was looking to unload these 120,000 bottles?

Similarly, what information did you give out? Did the representative of Continental Glass learn that:

_____ 1. Your normal supplier is Cactus Glass?

_____ 2. Cactus Glass is having labor problems?

_____ 3. You are trying to capture the holiday season market?

_____ 4. You need delivery within two weeks, and preferably in ten days?

_____ 5. You are willing to pay as much as 30 cents per bottle?

Still another way of viewing this negotiation is in terms of the potential for a long-term relationship. It is conceivable that you learned all of the aforementioned information about Continental Glass and still chose to settle at a midrange price because you do not want the company to discover that you have taken advantage of its situation. You want to develop goodwill, as Continental is a potential future supplier.

So, let's do a self-assessment, and ask your negotiating counterpart (the Continental Glass representative) to do the same. Think about this negotiation and answer these questions, being as specific as possible in your responses.

What do you think you did well in this negotiation?

1. ———————————————————————

2. ———————————————————————

3. ———————————————————————

4. ———————————————————————

5. ———————————————————————

What do you think you should do differently in the next negotiation?

1. ———————————————————————

2. ———————————————————————

3. ———————————————————————

4. ———————————————————————

5. ———————————————————————

What do you think the other representative did well in this negotiation?

1. ———————————————————————

2. ———————————————————————

3. ———————————————————————

4. ———————————————————————

5. ———————————————————————

What do you think the other representative should do differently in his or her next negotiation?

1. _____

2. _____

3. _____

4. _____

5. _____

Take a few minutes to share your perceptions, first by describing what you think you did well and getting feedback from the other negotiator about what he or she thought you did well. Then describe what you think you need to do differently next time. Again, get feedback from the other negotiator.

Did you find at any point that you got stuck arguing your respective positions? For example, one common sticking point is the quantity of bottles exchanged. You want 80,000 bottles, but the Continental Glass representative wants to unload 120,000. By discovering the reasons behind their need to sell 120,000 rather than 80,000 bottles (that is, their interest, which might be not to get stuck indefinitely with the extra 40,000 bottles), or sharing your interest in not having to store the bottles, you can find a win-win solution.

Finally, go back to the eight behaviors of successful negotiators described in the previous chapter. Which of these behaviors did you use effectively? Which of the behaviors do you think you could have used more effectively in this negotiation? You might want to pick one of the behaviors that you felt you could have used more effectively (asking questions, testing understanding and summarizing discussions, sharing internal motives, explaining your reasoning before disagreeing) and practice it over the next couple of days, or practice avoiding its use in the case of offering counterproposals; defending your

position and counterattacking; offering multiple, diluted arguments; or employing value statements (irritators). Practice is
the key. The more situations in which you employ a new
behavior, the more comfortable and confident you become in
using it.

7

Negotiation Styles

The most difficult thing in life is to know yourself.
—Thales, ancient Greek philosopher

Despite the uniqueness of each and every negotiation, we sometimes develop habits or preferences in approaching others during negotiations. These preferences can be grounded in our personalities, the behaviors learned from our mothers and fathers while we were growing up, or simply trial and error (some approaches worked better than others, so we kept using them).

Although everyone has some degree of flexibility in his or her approach to negotiation, some behaviors may be relied on more than others. If there is enough consistency in your actions across situations, then your friends, business associates, and others may come to recognize a pattern or style of negotiating.

Generally speaking, having a single strong and prevailing style is probably not what you want. It may mean that you lack the flexibility to adapt to unique situations. If the style is easily recognizable, it probably means that others have learned what to expect from you. As Napoleon once said, you do not want to use a tactic too frequently, lest your opponent learn the tactic (and how to counter it).

Let's see what we can learn about your negotiating preferences. Listed in this chapter are twenty pairs of statements regarding negotiating behavior. For each pair, you must distribute five points between the two statements, corresponding to the extent to which each statement reflects your behavior. For example, if we were asking about the foods that you eat (meat versus vegetables) and you are a vegetarian, you probably would distribute points as follows:

___
__0__ a. Meats

__5__ b. Vegetables
___

If you enjoyed both meats and vegetables but had a slight preference for meat, you might assign the points as follows:

___
__3__ a. Meats

__2__ b. Vegetables
___

Now let's push ourselves away from the dinner table and sit down at the bargaining-and-negotiation table. Think about your negotiation experiences overall. For each pair of behaviors shown below, assign numbers that total five for the pair.

1. _____ a. I try to help the other party, even if it means giving up my needs.
   _____ b. I exchange information and ideas freely.

2. _____ a. I try to find compromise solutions.
   _____ b. I look for and exploit the other party's weaknesses in a negotiation.

3. _____ a. I prefer to avoid contact with difficult negotiators.
   _____ b. I try to preserve the relationship at all costs.

4. _____ a. I try to collaborate.
   _____ b. I will back off my demands a little.

5. _____ a. I am competitive and try to ensure that my needs are met.
   _____ b. I prefer to avoid controversy.

6. _____ a. As a rule, I try to avoid negotiating.
   _____ b. I look for opportunities to split the difference in a negotiation.

7. _____ a. I let the other party dictate the terms of the agreement.
   _____ b. I press the logic of my position.

8. _____ a. I don't give up until I get what I want.
   _____ b. I try to satisfy both our needs.

9. _____ a. I will give something up for something in return.
   _____ b. I try to keep the other party happy.

10. _____ a. I seek to build trust.
    _____ b. I avoid situations that might create tension.

11. _____ a. I am usually willing to settle for a part of what I want.
    _____ b. I withhold information that might give the other party an advantage.

12. _____ a. I avoid open discussions of issues and concerns.
    _____ b. I try not to hurt the other person's feelings.

13. _____ a. I try to convince the other party that I am right.
    _____ b. I listen to the other person before sharing my views.

14. _____ a. I focus on the other party's concerns more than mine.
    _____ b. I will look for an intermediate position (halfway between our expectations).

15. _____ a. I try to bring issues or concerns into the open.
    _____ b. I avoid people who are tough negotiators.

16. _____ a. I go along with the other party's suggestions.
    _____ b. I use my power to influence the outcome of a negotiation.

17. _____ a. In every negotiation I look for opportunities where give-and-take can occur.
    _____ b. I look for creative solutions that make both parties winners.

18. _____ a. I try to outsmart and outtalk the other party.
    _____ b. I withdraw from negotiations, even when I might win.

19. _____ a. I try to deal with all the issues that are important to both of us.
    _____ b. I focus only on the issues that we agree on, not those issues of disagreement.

20. _____ a. I prefer to postpone facing difficult negotiations.
    _____ b. I will give up some of my demands if the other party will do the same.

Scoring Key

Transfer the number of points you assigned to each of the behaviors, beginning with 1a and 1b, to the corresponding spaces in Figure 7-1. Do this for all twenty pairs. Then total your score for each of the five columns.

Five Negotiation Styles

These five styles (or tactics, if they are used situationally) are defined by two dimensions: concern for your own self-interest (*substantive outcome*) and concern for the other party or the relationship (*relational outcome*).

Figure 7-1: Scoring Key for Your Negotiating Style

____ 2b	____ 1a	____ 1b	____ 3a	____ 2a
____ 5a	____ 3b	____ 4a	____ 5b	____ 4b
____ 7b	____ 7a	____ 8b	____ 6a	____ 6b
____ 8a	____ 9b	____10a	____10b	____ 9a
____11b	____12b	____13b	____12a	____11a
____13a	____14a	____15a	____15b	____14b
____16b	____16a	____17b	____18b	____17a
____18a	____19b	____19a	____20a	____20b
_____	_____	_____	_____	_____
Competing	Accommodating	Collaborating	Avoiding	Compromising

The Competing Style

As shown in Figure 7-2, the *competing* style focuses on self-interest or substantive outcome, generally at the expense of the other party and the relationship. It involves:

* Persisting until you get what you want
* Competing to ensure that your needs are met
* Trying to outsmart and outtalk the other party
* Using your power to influence the outcome of a negotiation
* Trying to convince the other party
* Withholding information that might give the other party an advantage
* Exploiting the other party's weaknesses in a negotiation

The Accommodating Style

The *accommodating* style is just the opposite of the competing style: concerned with preserving the relationship, even if it

Figure 7-2: Negotiation Styles

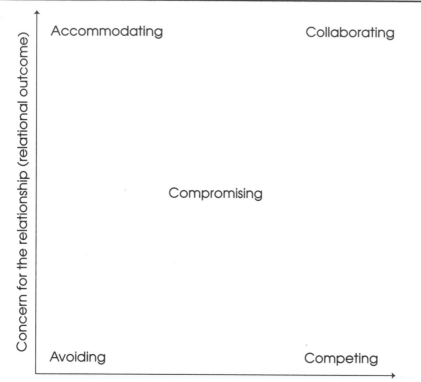

means giving up substantive outcome. Accommodating can include:

- ◆ Focusing on the other party's concerns more than your own
- ◆ Going along with the other party's suggestions
- ◆ Trying to help the other party even if it means giving up your own needs
- ◆ Trying to preserve the relationship at all costs
- ◆ Letting the other party dictate the terms of the agreement.
- ◆ Trying to keep the other party happy
- ◆ Trying not to hurt the other party's feelings
- ◆ Focusing on issues that you and the other party agree on rather than those issues of disagreement

The Collaborating Style

Collaboration involves exploring individual and mutual interests in an effort to satisfy everyone's needs. It is through collaboration that win-win solutions are possible. (Remember our negotiation involving the oranges?) This means:

- Bringing issues or concerns into the open·
- Dealing with issues that are important to both parties
- Looking for creative solutions that make both parties winners
- Listening to the other person before you share your views
- Seeking to build trust
- Seeking to satisfy the needs of both parties
- Exchanging information and ideas freely

The Avoiding Style

Avoiding involves simply that: avoiding not only the issues but the other party or parties and negotiation itself. This category also includes:

- Avoiding contact with difficult negotiators
- Avoiding controversy
- Avoiding situations that might create tension
- Avoiding open discussions of issues and concerns
- Withdrawing from negotiations, even when you might win
- Postponing facing difficult negotiations

In the case of the contested oranges, avoiding would occur if the thirsty party, seeking to avoid negotiation, grabbed a glass of water without discussing the matter or went to the market to buy some juice.

The Compromising Style

Finally, *compromising* is a partial-win, partial-lose proposition, where you get some of what you want but not everything, and likewise for the other party. This tactic or style includes:

- Splitting the difference
- Backing off on demands
- Giving up something for something in return
- Taking an intermediate position (halfway between expectations)
- Engaging in give-and-take

In the oranges negotiation, compromising involves dividing the oranges (for example, each person gets one of the two oranges).

Interpreting Your Score and Style

There are several ways to interpret your scores. One way is to look at the style that received the most points. If the number is significantly larger than for the other styles (40 points maximum for any single style), this suggests a preference for that style. If there are two or three styles that significantly exceed the others, then you have a preference for those styles. Likewise, is there a style that received very few points? This is a behavioral pattern you do not use very frequently. Generally speaking, you want to feel comfortable using all of these behaviors, because each has a time and place where it can be effective.

A second way of looking at these results is in terms of your orientation toward the two broader dimensions upon which the five styles are based: self-interest (substantive outcome) versus the other party or the relationship (relational outcome). Do you have a preference for one dimension over the other? Let's calculate your orientation toward these two dimensions (Figure 7-3). Which number is larger? By how much? This suggests a preference for one of these two dimensions over the other.*

How do you view your negotiating counterpart? Individuals with a strong concern for substantive outcomes might be likely to view the other party to a negotiation as an adversary or opponent, while individuals with a strong concern for a relational outcome might be likely to view the other party as a negotiating partner.

*Note that this calculation ignores your compromising score. The compromising style is neither high nor low in terms of concern for substantive outcome, and it is neither high nor low in terms of concern for relational outcome.

Figure 7-3: Calculating Your Orientations Towards Substantive Outcome and Relational Outcome

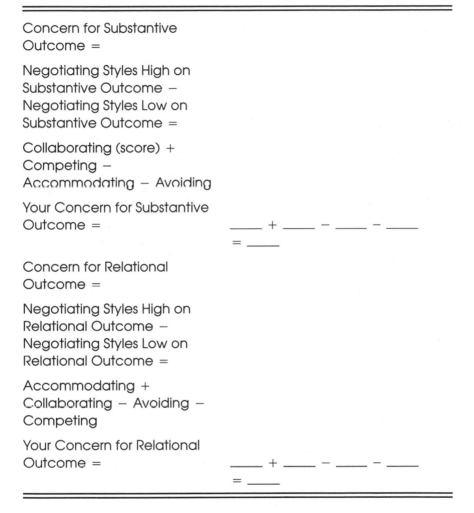

Concern for Substantive
Outcome =

Negotiating Styles High on
Substantive Outcome –
Negotiating Styles Low on
Substantive Outcome =

Collaborating (score) +
Competing –
Accommodating – Avoiding

Your Concern for Substantive
Outcome =   _____ + _____ – _____ – _____

              = _____

Concern for Relational
Outcome =

Negotiating Styles High on
Relational Outcome –
Negotiating Styles Low on
Relational Outcome =

Accommodating +
Collaborating – Avoiding –
Competing

Your Concern for Relational
Outcome =   _____ + _____ – _____ – _____

              = _____

Think for a moment of five different people (fictitious people, if you wish), each with a preference for a different one of the five negotiating styles. Which of the five people (styles) would you most like to encounter in a negotiation, and which would you least like to encounter?

I would *most* like to encounter someone whose style is:

_____

_____

_____

_____

_____

_____

I would *least* like to encounter someone whose style is:

_____

_____

_____

_____

_____

_____

If you are like most people, you don't want to encounter someone who is going to battle you every step of the way (competing) unless this is your own style, you are comfortable with this style, and you believe that you can win every time. Nor do you want someone, in most cases, who is going to avoid or withdraw. You would prefer to encounter an accommodating or collaborating approach, or someone who is flexible in orientation. What the accommodating and collaborating approaches have in common is concern for the other party or the relationship. You want your counterpart to be concerned about you and your best interests.

Recognizing the advantages of an accommodating or collaborative opponent, many negotiators try to create the sense of a relationship (present or future) even where none exists. They call you by your name—by your first name in many instances, or by your nickname. How can you get upset with someone who calls you by an endearing name? I once had a supervisor who made promises he did not keep, asked for my opinion but never gave his, employed task forces in name only, and worked behind the scenes to undo group decisions. But he always shook my hand, patted me on the back, gave me a smile, and referred to me as "Rog," so it was difficult to treat him as a person with a competing style.

Salespeople know all too well the importance of creating a sense of relationship. They act like your best friend, although you may never see them again once the sale is completed. They connect immediately by noticing the Denver Broncos cap that you are wearing, or by asking where you bought that beautiful coat or those boots. They laugh with you, commiserate with you, tell you stories, give you "inside" information, and call you by your first name. When negotiations get sticky, they say "Bob, help me out here. I want to do business with you. I want an agreement. Bob, help me make it happen." That sounds like a collaboration, doesn't it?

The treasurer of the organization described in the introduction of this book didn't just turn on the charm when the bank representative reported that neither of our names was on the signature card. His relaxed business attire, friendly introduction, and easygoing manner upon first engaging the representative created a special warmth and confidence (an I-feel-I've-known-you-all-my-life attitude) that set the stage for dealing with the absence of our signatures.

Maybe these are the makings of a real relationship between you and the person trying to sell you this automobile, or perhaps the camaraderie is an illusion. In either case, it is harder to be demanding or aggressive with a new friend, with someone who knows your uncle, with someone who roots for the Broncos, than with a nameless, faceless bill collector on the phone. For this reason alone, it is always a good idea to learn the other party's name and use it in your negotiations. It is polite and friendly, and it builds trust and collaboration. Doing so, especially in a telephone negotiation, not only allows you to add a touch of congeniality to an impersonal medium but also gives you a name to use if things run afoul and you need to call a second time. How many times have you reached a different representative when calling back, and this person has never heard of the offer that was made to you by someone else earlier? "Who did you talk to?" this representative asks. You can't remember. Try this in your next commercial phone call. Ask the person for his or her name and use it in your discussions. It is almost guaranteed to pave the way to a more fruitful negotiation.*

Finally, how would you respond to other negotiators who favor each of the five styles?

If the other negotiator favors:	My most likely response would be:
Competing	_____
Accommodating	_____
Collaborating	_____
Avoiding	_____
Compromising	_____

If you are like most people, your behavior varies depending on how another party approaches you. Individuals whom you

---

*I say "almost," because a word of caution is in order. Occasionally the other party perceives such familiarity to be inappropriate because of age or status differences. A good friend experienced this with a well-known, much-senior sports figure (actually, the owner of a sports team). Referring to him by his first name during a telephone conversation, my friend was quickly taken to task: "Do you know me? Have we met?" What the elder figure wanted was respect (to be referred to as Mr. X); giving it to him would have cost nothing and probably been a more effective route to negotiating an agreement.

routinely negotiate with have probably recognized this pattern and, depending on their preferences, choose an approach that works for them at some level. For example, if your typical response to a competing approach is to accommodate, negotiating intimates may learn that they can get their way by turning to a competing approach. If you respond to a collaborating approach with collaboration, this may be their first choice with you (since it preserves a sense of relationship), with compromising or competing as fallbacks. Negotiators who don't know you so well may try several different approaches as a means of testing how you respond to these various approaches—a way of profiling a negotiator with whom future negotiations are likely.

Negotiating styles—yours or another party's—can be difficult to change. Sometimes it is wise to look for a better match-up, rather than try to change someone's style or approach. Suppose, for example, you purchase some gift certificates from Ticketmaster that get lost in the mail. You call asking to have them reissued, but the person you speak to says this cannot be done without Ms. Johnson's approval, and she is not in today. You try to press your case, but the service representative puts you on hold. He finally comes back and says emphatically that he cannot help you without authorization. What do you do? One thing you can do is say "Thank you," hang up, and call back ten minutes later. Perhaps you will get someone with a different style and a different interpretation of policies. Chances are your approach will be different as well.

Your style of negotiating is just one aspect of your personality that can affect whether and how you approach others. Although not unrelated to negotiating styles, risk-taking propensity can influence your willingness to take chances—socially and financially. This is the subject of the next chapter.

8

Risky Business

You can't steal second base and keep one foot on first.
—Anonymous

Let's try a simple card game, one that a friend taught me years ago. He called it Indian Poker (perhaps because he was from India). It can be played with just two people, but it becomes more interesting with three, four, or five players.

Shuffle an ordinary deck of cards, and place the deck facedown between the players. Each player draws one card from the top of the deck, and without looking at it holds it on his forehead so that all the other players can see the face value (2 is low, ace is high). You can see what card(s) everyone else has, but not the card you have. Then, each person bets according to what he sees, not only in cards but in the expressions on the faces of the other players and their actions. You can play for pennies, nickels, quarters, matchsticks, whatever. Start out with fifteen coins or tokens each, and bet or fold (turn in your cards) according to what you see. After all but one person has folded, or someone calls the last bet to see all cards, the person with the highest card wins all the coins or tokens bet. Continue playing for seven or eight hands (rounds), or until someone has all the coins or tokens. Write down your outcome below.

Number of players: _____

Number of coins or tokens: _____

Final outcome: _____

This game is interesting because it contains a heavy element of bluffing and nonverbal communication. It is also about risk, beginning with what you and the other players agreed to play for (pennies, nickels, quarters, matchsticks, etc.). Beyond the stakes, though, how often did you fold? How often did you match someone's bid or raise the bid? Did you find yourself folding when you had a king or an ace? What was your immediate behavior in the subsequent round after you lost? What happened when you got ahead on coins or tokens? What happened when you were low on coins or tokens? In the end, how did you feel about winning or losing? Who were the people you played with, and how did your relationship to the other player(s) affect the way you felt about winning or losing? How might you play the game differently if each of you had 100 pennies or tokens? If one of you had 100 pennies or tokens and the other party (parties) had only 10 tokens?

It is, of course, just a game—but it is a game with some risks. The risks are personal (saving face, reputation, public image) as well as financial (low finance, rather than high finance), just as they often are in negotiation.

If you are like most people, you would like to reduce, if not eliminate, most risks. Forget it, or at least the elimination of risk. Risk, like negotiation, is a condition of life. When you ride on a bus or an airplane, buy food at the supermarket, approach a neighbor's dog, drink water from the tap, tell a friend about a movie, put your name on a business report, or ask someone for a date or a favor, you are taking a chance.

Obviously, some risks are far less perilous than others, for you and for those parties who might be affected by your behavior. Yet some people are generally more comfortable taking risks than others, whether it be asking someone for a date or exercising the determination and deception of nuclear brinkmanship.

The degree of comfort you have as a risk taker clearly influences the process and outcome of your negotiations. If you are not willing to take risks, when others are capable and willing to do so, you may be at a disadvantage. If you are reluctant to ask your supervisor for a new computer, for example, while others in the organization are confident and bold in their requests, you may not get a new computer under any circumstances, let alone when the budget is tight and only one or two new computers can be purchased.

In reality, there are several types of risk in negotiation. First and foremost is the risk of asking for what you want. "You can't get someone's vote if you don't ask for it," was a rule that Tip O'Neill, former Speaker of the House, preached and practiced. Yet I have encountered friends (and on a few occasions been there myself) for whom asking to substitute one item for another on a menu, asking for a donation, asking for another application form, asking for the correct time, asking for an autograph, or asking for directions was a major obstacle. Many of us are often far more comfortable asking for something on behalf of someone else than asking for the same thing for ourselves.

A second type of risk concerns potential financial loss. Risk avoiders are afraid of risking any loss; risk-averse individuals want a higher potential return on their capital ventures. How might you play Indian Poker if all the players have 100 tokens? If everyone has 10 tokens? If you have 100 tokens and everyone else has 10 tokens? If you have 10 tokens and everyone else has 100 tokens? For some people, it does not matter what their stake is; they are reluctant to wager more than a small fraction for fear of financial loss.

A third type of risk occurs as the result of incomplete or erroneous information. The sports fan who bets on a team without first checking the injury list falls into this category, as does the employer who fails to check out a candidate's references, the home buyer who consciously forgoes a professional inspection, and the consumer who consistently takes the first product she sees. It may be due to laziness or indifference. Or it could be due to irrational optimism (which appears to be the case every time Charlie Brown is offered another chance to kick the football, only to have Lucy pull it away at the last second—for the umpteenth time). Whatever the reason, there are some individuals who take risks they know can be reduced with little more than a phone call, but they rush to a decision nonetheless.

There are many possible explanations for one's risk-taking proclivity, or lack thereof. It could have to do with self-esteem, family upbringing, cultural heritage, or situational factors. Many people who grew up during the Great Depression, for example, came to believe that saving—whether money, metal, paper, or bottles—was both a necessity and a virtue. Certainly if there is a precedent for risk taking, or if you have faced a situation before and summoned the courage, it is likely to be easier to hold hands again, ask a friend if you can borrow some *more* money, or walk away from an offer knowing that you have no comparable alternative.

Within a financial context, there are some additional indicators you might use to assess your degree of risk taking:

❖ Are more than half of your assets primarily in common stocks, commodity futures, or derivatives rather than savings, checking and money market accounts, or certificates of deposit?

❖ Are more than half your assets financed with debt (such as credit cards and other loans)?

❖ Do you ever play the lottery, gamble in Las Vegas, or bet on a golf game, wagering more than one one-thousandth of your personal assets?

❖ Is your life insurance worth less than twice your annual salary?

❖ Have you voluntarily resigned from a job more than three times within the past fifteen years (assuming you have been in the workforce more than fifteen years)?

The more often you answer yes to these questions, the more of a risk taker you are.

Given this discussion, you probably have a pretty good sense of what kind of risk taker you are. If I ask you to put an X on the line below, indicating overall what kind of a risk taker you are, you can probably do it without a lot of thought.

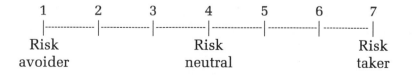

It should be noted, however, that individuals tend to inflate slightly their self-assessment of risk, since risk taking is viewed in most circles as a desirable characteristic, particularly among males (consider all the adventure heroes, from Teenage Mutant Ninja Turtles, Power Rangers, and X-Men to the Indiana Jones and James Bond characters in films). Also, risk avoiders tend to be more consistent in their behavior than those individuals who are risk takers.

Just because you are risk-averse does not mean that you cannot be an effective negotiator. However, you may require more information, and you probably will want to have a BATNA for crucial negotiations. If your risk aversion includes having a strong avoiding or accommodating negotiating style, you will want to practice engaging others in simple negotiations—asking for things that you would normally let pass, in retail settings and elsewhere. Starting simply, you can begin to build some additional confidence in a whole range of common, everyday negotiations.

You might be wondering how the negotiating styles described in Chapter 7 relate to your risk-taking tendencies. Recall the two dimensions that defined the negotiating styles: concern for self-interest (substantive outcome) and concern for the relationship (relational outcome). Some individuals have a strong orientation toward one or the other dimension, just as some individuals are strong risk avoiders and others are strong risk takers. These two characteristics can be combined to describe four negotiator temperaments (Figure 8-1).

Individuals who are risk avoiders (that is, preferring to avoid risk altogether, not just manage it) and who also have a strong preference for realizing self-interest (substantive outcome) tend to view negotiations as a zero-sum game or fixed pie—the larger the piece of the pie that one side receives, the less pie remains for the other side. If this type of negotiator presumes that the other party thinks the same way, then she is probably more concerned about what might be lost personally than what might be gained collectively. Consequently, this type of negotiator's temperament is distrustful, self-protective, and calculating. Chandler, from the TV sitcom "Friends," may well exhibit this temperament.

Risk avoiders who have a strong orientation toward maintaining relationships (relational outcome) are fearful of jeopar-

Figure 8-1: Negotiator Temperaments

	Substantive-outcome orientation	Relational-outcome orientation
Risk avoider	Distrustful Self-protective Calculating	Indulgent Conforming Accepting
Risk taker	Aggressive Demanding Dominating	Supportive Endearing Engaging

dizing those relationships, new ones as well as those already established. They are afraid of saying the wrong thing, offending others, and causing loss of face. As a result, their negotiating disposition or temperament tends to be indulgent of others, conforming, and accepting. This is Charlie Brown from the Peanuts comic strip.

Risk takers with a preference for substantive outcome are willing to "break a few eggs in order to make an omelet." They often don't think or see what implications their actions are having on others. All they can think about is the omelet. They are the Tom Cruise character (the hustler Charlie Babbitt) from the movie *Rainman* and Kramer from the television show "Seinfeld." By temperament, they are both more inclined to be aggressive, demanding, dominating.

Finally, risk takers who are oriented toward relational outcomes are intent on building and nurturing relationships, even if it is not clear what advantage is in it for them. They believe that relationships are the fabric of life. Their tendency is to be supportive, endearing, and engaging. They includes Jessica Fletcher, from the TV series "Murder, She Wrote," and Oprah Winfrey, the talk show host.

Think back to the challenge you were given in Chapter 1, to

go to a restaurant and order something that is not on the menu. How might individuals of these temperaments approach this negotiation? A substantive-oriented risk avoider is probably concerned that she is going to be charged extra for the special order; she does not want to give up anything in the negotiation. A relational-oriented risk avoider may be reluctant to ask for anything unusual, fearful that the waitperson will be annoyed or that his companions will be embarrassed. Any request from this type of negotiator is probably for something simple (maybe cheese on his scrambled eggs). Among risk takers, a substantive-oriented risk taker would make his demand challenging; he is the customer and the customer is always right. The relational-oriented risk taker would feel comfortable in conversation with the waitperson, building an acquaintance as a basis for requesting something special.

Does one of these four temperaments describe your approach to negotiation in most situations? Do you recognize the temperament of your spouse, a coworker, or a close friend? Keep in mind that these temperaments are based on a strong concern for self-interest versus relationship, and on either risk-taking or risk-avoiding tendencies (some people are risk-neutral). Not everyone is described by one of these four temperaments. An individual (yourself included) may not have a strong orientation along either of these two dimensions. Also, an individual can have a change of temperament, as Charlie Babbitt did in *Rainman*.

Sometimes it is useful to engage in role reversal as a way of gaining perspective on your own temperament and those of others. For example, if your temperament favors being a substantive-oriented risk avoider (distrustful, self-protective, calculating), then try playing the exact opposite—a relational-oriented risk taker (supportive, endearing, engaging). You can even reenact my earlier challenge to go to a restaurant and order something not on the menu. Pick a new restaurant, and try out an opposite temperament. How does it feel?

If you are like most people, you probably prefer not to encounter someone who is aggressive, demanding, and dominating. In Chapter 12, I address the problem of dealing with tough negotiators. Next, though, I introduce some common negotiating tactics and offer suggestions on how to counter each of them.

9

Eight Common Tactics and Their Countermeasures

The height of cleverness is being able to conceal it.
—François La Rochefoucauld (1613–1680)

Although we sometimes use the terms *behaviors* and *tactics* interchangeably, they do not carry the same connotation, at least for many people. The behaviors of successful negotiators (Chapter 5) are especially useful in pursuing win-win outcomes. They fall into a category of behaviors we might think of as *collaborative*—concerned with both personal and mutual interests. Tactics also are behaviors, but they constitute a special category that generally is more concerned with personal interests or self-interest than with the interests of the other party or the relationship.

Tactics are useful because you may choose to employ them in a variety of situations, and even if you choose not to do so, it is helpful to be able to recognize what tactics others are using to their advantage and how to respond to them. Since tactics are often employed at crucial stages in a negotiation, they represent potential turning points. An adroit, tactful response is generally preferred to meeting the other party head-on (for example, calling him on using a particular tactic) or severing relations straightaway.

Eight Common Negotiation Tactics

Described next are eight common tactics used in business and social negotiations, and one or more countermeasures for each that you might consider if the tactic is used on you.

Exaggerated First Offer

Asking questions is one way of inviting the other party to share information with you, a means of determining how you can help (or hurt) this person. Generally, however, your opponent is not going to come right out and say how much she can spend, unless she believes the offer is well below the market value of the desired goods or services. If you have ever tried to trade in your car, you have experienced this. Car dealers invariably make the first offer on a trade-in (typically after you have decided on a new car)—and for a fraction of your car's Blue Book value.

Making an exaggerated first offer (high or low), or at least what seems exaggerated to you, is another way to gather information by checking the reaction of the other party. It could be surprise, disappointment, nonchalance, acceptance, or enthusiasm—each suggesting a different expectation and course of action. Some foreknowledge of how well the other party knows the market value of a proposal could be useful, because it allows you to predict or gauge the response.

Even if the other party refuses your first offer, this tactic could work to your advantage. If the first offer happens to be within the realm of what is acceptable, the offer likely serves as an anchor around which bargaining will center. Most parties recognize this, so they make an offer at least slightly higher or lower than where they want to settle, even employing an odd number in the vicinity of an expected final settlement. For example, if you want to sell for $1,000, you ask for $1,100, hoping that the rounder number ($1,000) ends up as the settlement price.

Of course, going with an exaggerated first offer could offend the other party. You never know, unless you've scouted the other party's position prior to face-to-face negotiating. Or this person might simply be putting on an act, hoping to move you away from the initial offer by appearing shocked or offended. Much depends on how far afield the offer is and also the other party's alternatives to a negotiated agreement. If you have no information on the other party, or believe that she has few if any alternatives, this tactic could prove helpful.

Countermeasures: One way of dealing with this tactic is to be the first to use it. If you make the first offer, you create the anchor. By exaggerating your "demands," you may be able to learn something from the other party's immediate nonverbal behavior.

If the other party makes the first offer, be careful what you signal. An outrageous demand from your opponent could seem quite satisfactory to you, but it might be better to show surprise or disbelief. Or change the subject, moving to a different issue. This signals to your counterpart that the offer is not acceptable, while allowing everyone to save face. It also allows you to use some other tactics discussed later in this chapter (for example, investment).

Speed-Ups

In the movie *Kramer vs. Kramer*, Dustin Hoffman plays Ted Kramer, whose wife (played by Meryl Streep) leaves him and their son, Billy, only to return months later to reclaim Billy. Desperate to maintain custody of his son, Ted needs to secure employment after suddenly losing his job just before the custody hearing is to begin. He visits an advertising agency on the Friday before Christmas to present his portfolio for a position for which he is clearly overqualified. The principals in the company are impressed with his work, but they are in the midst of a holiday party and would like to think things over and get back to him. "No," Ted says, "this is a one-day-only offer, gentlemen. If you really want me, you make your decision right now." After a brief, private meeting, they call Ted back in and welcome him aboard.

Haste makes waste. It also makes for lopsided negotiations. If you are in a hurry, you often don't think through your options carefully, let alone check them out or develop additional options. You don't ask the kind of detailed questions that tell you whether or not this negotiated agreement meets all your needs.

You don't ask the broad questions that determine why the other party is negotiating with you. In fact, you send a message to the other party—valid or otherwise—that you do not have lots of options.

Knowing this, some negotiating opponents set arbitrary deadlines and speed up negotiations to gain an advantage. They even manipulate speech patterns to that end, talking quickly and employing short, abrupt sentences. Many airlines use the deadline technique when they tell you that to secure the quoted rate you must buy your ticket within twenty-four hours—a ticket that is nonrefundable and subject to penalties if you wish to make any changes. Other commercial enterprises accomplish the same effect through qualifiers such as "while supplies last" or "for a limited time only."

Speeding up the pace of a face-to-face negotiation can tell you a lot about the position of the other party, especially if his pace speeds up to match yours.

Countermeasures: There are several things you can do to avoid becoming the victim of a drive-by negotiation. Sometimes the other party is simply anxious, for any number of reasons. Asking if you can get back to him at a specific time later that day or by a specific day later that week may satisfy his need to know that something is going to happen, and buy yourself a wedge of time to clear your head, rethink your options, or talk with a friend.

If the other party is in more of a hurry, you are probably better off sharing internal motives or feelings about the speed of the negotiation. You might even offer to help find ways of relieving the deadline. But if shifting the discussion to the process of the negotiation rather than the content doesn't change both the focus and tenor of the negotiation, you are wise to consider passing on this opportunity (that is, exercising your BATNA).

Delays

Conversely, slowing down or delaying a negotiation can unnerve an opponent. Delaying is a way of gaining information about the other party's sense of urgency. You say, "Thanks for your time. Can I get back to you in a week or two?" Or, if it is unclear who will get back to whom, you wait. How long does it take before the other party calls you? Delaying should tell you something about how important and urgent the deal is. In fact, this is one of the tactics that Ellen Fein and Sherrie Schneider suggest in their book *The Rules: Time-Tested Secrets for Capturing the Heart of Mr. Right*. Rule number five is "Don't call him, and rarely return his calls." Delaying suggests that you have better things to do . . . you have options. The speed and frequency with which a suitor calls you says something about his or her options.

A second form of delay is shown in the proverbial expression "the check is in the mail." This type of delay is designed to make you feel secure in the moment, but after a week passes and nothing has arrived in the mail, you are left to figure out what it all means. Maybe the check got lost in the mail. Maybe it was never sent.

Countermeasures: For the first type of delay, you have several options, depending upon how important it is for you to have a commitment from this party at this time. If you truly are pressed (that is, you have no BATNA), you may want to try to determine the source of the delay by asking the other party directly. Perhaps you can help allay the fear or remove the stumbling block that is behind the delay. The inquiry should be made tactfully, of course, and there should be more curiosity and helpfulness than exasperation in your voice.

If you already have an acceptable BATNA, you might want to share this with the delaying party, particularly if you feel that you need to make a decision. Share this information in a way that suggests you are doing him a favor, letting him in on something, rather than as a threat or an ultimatum. Again, it is a win-win outcome that you desire. (Caution: Commenting that you have another potential date for Saturday night when the person you've just asked out inquires if she can get back to you later in the day is a relationship killer.)

Whether you have a BATNA or not, negotiate the length of the delay. Be specific about the day and time the other party will get back to you, summarizing your understanding orally or in writing. Be clear concerning what might happen in the interim (for example, you might accept a better offer), and use that time to establish or strengthen your BATNA. If the day and time arrive and the other party doesn't call or asks for another delay, it is time to exercise your options.

With the second type of delay ("It's in the mail"), your action is determined by your long-term relationship with the other party, how many times the check has been in the mail, and what is at risk. In the worst case, you have to find a way to help or hurt the other party (our Golden Rule). This could include everything from offering to stop by and pick up the check to filing a legal claim.*

Drawing Lines

Another common tactic of bargainers is creating an artificial bottom line. "I'm sorry, I can't go any lower than that. It is my bottom line." Often, we assume that this limit was established by someone else with equal or greater authority (spouse, supervisor, company policy), or that it is based on precedence (see authority limits section). Consequently, we accept the line drawn in the sand, and we don't cross it. The representative from Continental Glass says "I can't sell you fewer than 120,000 bottles" or "I cannot go any lower than 20 cents per bottle for a rush order." Using odd numbers, such as 21.5 cents per bottle, can add further credibility to an offer.

Similar to the bottom line is demarcating what is negotiable from what is not. In fact, it may be best to come right out and establish these boundaries, first by saying what is negotiable and then what is not negotiable: "All of the machinery and outbuildings are negotiable, but the horses are not for sale." By taking charge and following this sequence, you hold the other party's attention with "the good news" (here is what is negotiable) before clarifying what is not negotiable. You might even precede your declaration of what is not negotiable with an explanation

---

*A friend related a story from her younger days, when she was given promises regarding payment for consulting services she'd delivered but for which she had never been paid. Finally, she decided to go to the company and demand payment. Ultimately, the company's vice president for finance was called in to tell her that the company had no money to pay her. Her response was that she wasn't going to leave until she got paid. And she meant it. The vice president found the money.

("All the machinery and outbuildings are negotiable. The horses belong to my wife and she wants to keep them."), as with the explaining-before-disagreeing behavior described in Chapter 5.

Countermeasures: A frontal assault on someone's bottom line is likely to threaten or embarrass him (losing face, if he simply caves in). There may be occasions where this works, but a better approach is to employ a little negotiation jujitsu. Redirect the negotiation to focus on other issues or items that are important to this person (for example, various pieces of machinery). Negotiate those. Now the other party has an incentive (something to lose) if he doesn't back away from that bottom line and complete the negotiation.

With the second variation of this tactic—drawing lines around what is negotiable and what is not—the best approach might be to take control yourself by establishing the boundaries early on. If the other party has already taken the initiative, however, then you have a couple of options. Assuming that the nonnegotiable items or issues are of some value to you, find out why they are valuable to the other party—and just how valuable. The answer to "Why?" might provide the insight for a breakthrough, win-win solution. A second approach is to negotiate all those items that are on the table, perhaps to the advantage of this party, building momentum and commitment. Then, before the deal can be closed, you bring up the items or issues that were nonnegotiable. Much depends, of course, on how nonnegotiable those items or issues really are.

Creating Competition

This tactic hearkens back to our Golden Rule of negotiation: People will not negotiate with you unless they believe you can help them or hurt them. In every sector of the economy there exists competition for your business. J. C. Penney, Sears, K-Mart, and WalMart are all competing for pretty much the same clientele. AT&T, MCI, and Sprint all want to be your long-distance carrier. Delta, American, United, TWA, USAir, Midwest, Southwest, and Northwest are in a highly competitive market. They know this (although it doesn't hurt for you to remind them occasionally).

By creating competition for your money, you push them to give you their best offer. Many times there is considerable latitude and flexibility available to meet or match other offers.

When I had another telephone line installed in my home, I had the opportunity to choose a long-distance carrier. MCI already was my carrier, and after getting information and an offer from AT&T, I went back to MCI with their offer. Ultimately, I chose MCI again, but by some dumb luck, they got my order fouled up. No, this MCI representative had never heard of the rebate package I thought that I had been promised. Of course, I had neglected to get the name of the representative who made the offer—a nasty mistake. At that point, I expressed my disappointment and said I would just have to switch all my long-distance service over to AT&T. Guess what? The MCI representative had another package that he could offer me, of greater value than the original deal!

A good friend told me how he actually turned an unfavorable real estate market to his advantage through a creative twist on this tactic. During a seller's market, when real estate agents were showing homes to dozens of prospective buyers, my savvy friend identified six or eight houses in a neighborhood where he wanted to live—houses that were not for sale. He then sent letters to each owner, indicating that theirs was one of six houses he was interested in buying within a specified price range. Suddenly, the seller's market became a buyer's market for him as each owner contemplated being the one whose house he would buy (minus the expense of a 6 percent real estate agent's commission, I might add). Needless to say, he got his house.

What were those fundamental questions of negotiation again?

Countermeasures: The first thing to keep in mind when someone uses this tactic is that he is still talking to you. Why has this person taken the time to contact you, and why is he still talking to you? If your competitor has such a superior product or service, what is there to negotiate?

Obviously, there is something that he doesn't like about your competitor—or something about you, your product, your service, or your location that is appealing. In short, he believes that there is some way to be helped or hurt by you (the Golden Rule). One approach is to restate this party's concerns and wait to see if more information is forthcoming: "You would like 1,000 copies at a 20 percent discount, and you would like quick processing." In addition, if you are knowledgeable about your competitors, you might matter-of-factly point out the differences between their product and yours: "Yes, but their LP3 model does not do color printing, and the copy resolution is poorer." Finally, if you have alternatives, you can politely say, "I'm sorry, but we just cannot match that offer. What about 10 percent?"

Concessions

While on a business trip to Hawaii, a woman was killing time in one of the bazaars until she was to join some friends for dinner. Wandering from one vendor to the next, many of whom appeared to carry identical merchandise, she paused to inspect a sundress. Almost immediately, the proprietor approached her:

Proprietor: Do you like the dress?
Customer: It's very pretty. How much is it?
P: Fifty dollars, but for you, I will sell it for forty.
C: (taking one more look at the dress before putting it back) Hmm.
P: You like the dress? I will give it to you for thirty.
C: (returning to inspect the dress) What is it made of? Cotton?
P: (displaying the label) Yes, cotton.
C: Will the colors fade . . . or run?
P: No, no.
C: (shaking her head) I don't know.
P: Okay, twenty dollars.
C: Hmm. How about fifteen?
P: No. Twenty.
C (deciding against the dress, puts it back one last time and begins to walk away)
P: OK, fifteen.

This scenario is played out thousands of times every day in the bazaars and informal markets around the world. It is a social ritual. And this particular vendor has probably sold the same dress (or a similar version) for fifty dollars, ten dollars, and every price in between.

Because we all like to think that we got a deal, sellers often use concessions in combination with an inflated opening price as one of their tactics. Sometimes the initial price is only marginally inflated, and other times the price is grossly exaggerated. Besides price, there are a host of additional issues that one party might concede to another to close a deal: quantity, color, delivery date, shipping charges, accessories, wrapping or packaging, etc. Sometimes the concessions seem as valuable as the item for sale: "If you buy this revolutionary new ab machine now, we will throw in a free video on diet and exercise, plus a pedometer!" With such advertisements, it is easy to lose sight of our first fundamental question of negotiation—*What do I want?*—and buy on quantity rather than quality.

Countermeasures: Countermeasures might be the wrong word in the case of this tactic, since you certainly don't want to discourage the other party from making concessions. In fact, you hope to ensure that you get the product or service you want at the best total cost to you. However, there are several things to take note of regarding the use of this tactic, nuances that can help you read the other party's behavior as well as suggestions for how you might use concessions.

1. Pay attention to the timing of concessions. In the Hawaiian sundress story, the proprietor's opening offer included a concession. With many other vendors in the immediate area selling identical merchandise, the proprietor had to find a way to hold the attention of the prospective buyer. Generally speaking, an early concession signals lots of room for bargaining and negotiation.

2. Next, pay attention to the increments of the concessions. In this case, the first three increments were all ten dollars. This pattern suggests that the seller was not close to approaching her bottom line. If the second offer had been thirty, quite a different

settlement range and bottom line would have been communicated. Therefore, if you are the seller, you want any successive concessions you make to decrease around your settlement price. (Keep in mind that successive ten-dollar concessions represent a greater percentage for the buyer than for the seller. For example, the difference between forty dollars and thirty represents a 25 percent decline for the seller but a 33 percent difference for the buyer.)

3. Finally, watch for a range of concessions. If the seller suggests a settlement range as an initial offer (for example, "I would like between forty and fifty.") rather than a step-down concession such as used by the proprietor in this case ("Fifty dollars, but for you I will sell it for forty."), the seller is likely signaling less willingness to make concessions beyond this initial, built-in concession. That is, the seller implicitly is saying that she would like fifty but will sell for forty. Don't expect much movement below forty. If you are the prospective buyer, a good countermeasure is to change the topic from price to other issues, gathering additional information and creating an investment of time and energy on the part of the seller. The seller is likely to drop the settlement-range tactic and come back with a different, lower price later in the negotiation.

By the way, this same principle applies to the situation where you are offering your salary expectations to a prospective employer. If you say that your expectation is for a salary between $38,000 and $39,000, don't be surprised when the employer offers something in this range especially if the offer falls at or below what she was hoping to pay you. In fact, you probably will get something closer to $39,000.*

---

*As one final illustration of how concessions can be deceiving, consider the classic department store ad in which the price of all men's and women's designer clothing is reduced 30 percent, and an additional 20 percent off if you bring in the special coupon found in today's newspaper. At first blush, this looks like 50 percent off. But more often than not it is 30 percent off the original price and 20 percent off the discounted price (not the original price) for a total of 44 percent off. Specifically,

Effective discount = (first rate + second rate) − (first rate × second rate)
= (.30 + .20) − (.30 × .20)
= (.50) − (.06)
= .44

Investment

Despite the concept of sunk cost (which says that once you have spent your time or money on something you should consider that money spent . . . gone . . . sunk), everybody hates to lose an investment. We want to get a return, even if it means investing more time and money to achieve a return on the investment.

Nowhere is this more obvious than in federal spending. Time after time the federal government, for example, contracts with defense manufacturers for airplanes, missiles, tanks, and the like, each costing millions of dollars. The construction invariably takes longer than was scheduled and entails enormous cost overruns. Then, the manufacturers go back to Congress and ask for more money. And Congress appropriates it. Why? In part because the contract allows for some cost overruns, but also because the federal government wants to show something for its investment, and completion of the airplane or missile or tank is nigh.

Television producers use this principle of investment in scheduling commercials. During the network showing of a feature-length movie, you get the first half-hour commercial-free, during which you begin to get interested in the characters and the story line. Thereafter, the commercials come every fifteen minutes. By the end of the movie you have made such an investment that you are willing to endure commercials every ten minutes to find out how the movie ends. By an odd coincidence, the same is true with professional basketball and football broadcasts. All those time-outs (which map into commercials) are expended near the end of the game when everything is on the line. You've followed the game this long, you have to know who will win. After the game is over and you want to see the highlights hear the final statistics and analysis, and see and hear interviews with the stars of the game, there are more frequent and longer commercials between segments.

The identical principle applies when you go to a clothing store to buy a new suit or outfit. The sales person invests time in showing you this style or that style. You try on one, but you do not like the fit. You try on another, but the color doesn't seem right. You shift your interests from a suit to a sport coat. This salesperson, who is paid on commission, has now invested fifteen, twenty, thirty minutes in helping you try on and evaluate clothes. Other customers have wandered in and out of the store during this time. The salesperson wants to sell you something—wants a return on investment, in this case, an investment of time.

Creating investments can give you an advantage in negotiating, since salespeople and others often provide inducements to ensure some return on their investment (for example, a discount, free alterations, one-day alterations, a garment bag, a free tie). Simply recognizing the investment(s) that someone has made can be equally effective. A friend who was trying to sell her condo ran into trouble when a misunderstanding arose regarding the parking space, which she wanted to sell separately. The prospective buyer—the only buyer she really had—was threatening to back out over this parking space, citing financial reasons. However, the buyer had not only invested time and money into looking for a place to buy but also applied for a mortgage (an additional investment of time and money) and locked into a mortgage rate. As rates suddenly rose, there was an added incentive to close the deal (which he quickly did when the seller suggested that she might not sell the condo).

Countermeasures: The best antidote here is probably a BATNA. If you are the seller and the negotiation is dragging on, excuse yourself to attend to another customer, client, or project. This sends the message that you are a busy person and you have alternatives. You might also create a sense of competition and urgency. Indicate to the customer that this is the last item in this color remaining in the store. Prices are likely to go up next week. Play up another prospective buyer's interest in the same item. If you are the buyer (as in the condo case), you might look for or move on other properties (that is, expand your options). Alternatively, you can withhold payments, threaten suit, or terminate the contract.

Authority Limits

Authority limits can occur in a number of forms, all of which are wonderful for holding the line or buying you more time.

One form of authority limit comprises organizational policies, procedures, and rules. You go into a bookstore to return a book someone bought for you as a gift (since you already own a copy of this book) only to discover that the store has a no-returns policy. "See," says the clerk, pointing to a sign behind the counter. You arrive at the airport for a domestic flight and discover long lines. Off to the right is an agent handling international flights and preferred customers only, and there is no line. With a sigh, you head to one of the domestic lines.

Most of us are very dutiful about obeying authority, particularly policies put in writing. We "Keep off the grass," "Keep out," "Do not enter," "Knock before entering," "Form a single line," "Walk," "Don't walk," limit ourselves to "One per customer," and "Do not remove this label under penalty of fine or imprisonment." We dutifully check out at 11:00 A.M. because that is the hotel's policy. Keep in mind, however, that anything that was negotiated (as most policies, procedures, and rules were) is negotiable.

Reprinted with special permission of King Features Syndicate.

A second type of authority limit involves a third party who must be consulted. This is a favorite of car salespeople. You are negotiating the purchase of a new car. It has been an exhaustive process, but you believe that finally you have found the car that truly meets your needs. With some trepidation you have negotiated everything from price to warranty to air conditioning to color. It is the package you want. The salesperson agrees but has to check with the manager. You cringe. The salesperson goes into a back room. Maybe you can see the salesperson talking to "the manager," maybe not. Hours pass (or so it seems). The salesperson finally returns and says the manager needs $500 more. You are this close. What do you do?

Using a third party—a boss, supervisor, manager, business partner, spouse—as an authority limit not only keeps a party from giving away the store but is a way of testing eagerness, whether a legitimate authority exists or not. It makes negotiating more complicated for you since the more people with whom you must negotiate, the more needs and expectations must be met. If you cannot meet and negotiate face-to-face with a third party, you lose access to a great deal of verbal and nonverbal information.

Countermeasures: Although not always the case, it is generally true that if you don't ask for something, you won't get it.* Hence, there is nothing wrong with asking about a policy, procedure, or rule (or seeking to circumvent it). In many cases, simply acknowledging (indeed, respecting) the other party's hierarchical authority is all he or she is asking for. The airlines do not want you to wait in long lines; it is bad for business. Going up to the international or preferred customer check-in and asking

---

*By way of illustration, I was once shopping in the "social" Safeway in Washington, D.C. (where people actually dress up to shop), when I spotted Donna Shalala, secretary of health and human services, in among the vegetables. Previously, she served as the chancellor of the University of Wisconsin-Madison (UW), where I went to graduate school. She was and still is a big supporter of the University of Wisconsin and in fact owned a dog named for the mascot of the school, Bucky Badger. Without hesitation I went up to her: "You look like someone who would have a dog named Bucky." She hardly looked up. I told her that I had gone to the university and was now teaching in Washington. She made a polite comment, never interrupting her shopping, and then turned away.

I was deflated. I thought of all the possible excuses: she was with someone, in a hurry, wanting to keep her "private" life private. Dejected, I continued my shopping until an idea struck me. One of my dearest friends, a graduate, former employee, and longtime UW backer, was gravely ill with cancer. What a lift she would get from a card signed by Donna Shalala. But I couldn't ask. I couldn't face rejection again.

Finally, though, I went to the card section of the store and picked out a get-well card. Then, back through the store I went before I found Shalala near a cereal display. I apologized for bothering her again but explained that I had a very sick friend who had given years of service to UW and would love a card signed by her. My tone was somber and serious, just like my mission. Her attitude was suddenly equally somber and cooperative. She asked my friend's name, borrowed my pen, pulled down a cereal box to write on, and wrote a touching message. I was thrilled, and my sick friend loved the card. But it never would have occurred had I not overcome my initial embarrassment, changed my tone, and asked.

"Can I check in here for a domestic flight?" is likely to be met with the utmost receptivity. Remember, anything that was negotiated is negotiable, and organizational policies, procedures, and rules were negotiated by a small group of employees, many of whom have probably long since left the company. These rules are not among the laws of nature.

In any negotiation, but particularly those in which considerable time or money is at stake, determine at the outset if your negotiating counterpart has the authority to negotiate an agreement. There is no point and certainly no joy in having to negotiate twice (unless you want and need the practice). Insist on negotiating with the party or parties who are authorized to close the deal and sign a contract. If this tactic takes you by surprise, look for some literature to read, or pull out that book you have been reading, to pass the time. A good friend uses this countermeasure frequently, and when the delay is protracted he asks the returning salesperson to wait until he has finished the section or chapter he is reading.

Comfort and Competency With These Tactics

These are eight tactics commonly used in business and social negotiations. Now, let's take a moment to assess your comfort level and competency in using each tactic. How frequently do you think you use each of them? Indicate your comfort and frequency of use by placing an *X* on each of the scales shown below.

Tactic	*Use*		
Exaggerated first offer	|-------------------------------	-------------------------------	----------------------------------- |
	Very infrequent	Moderately frequent	Very frequent
Speed-ups	|-------------------------------	-------------------------------	----------------------------------- |
	Very infrequent	Moderately frequent	Very frequent
Delays	|-------------------------------	-------------------------------	----------------------------------- |
	Very infrequent	Moderately frequent	Very frequent

Drawing lines	|----------------------------|----------------------------|
	Very	Moderately	Very
	infrequent	frequent	frequent

Creating competition	|----------------------------|----------------------------|
	Very	Moderately	Very
	infrequent	frequent	frequent

Concessions	|----------------------------|----------------------------|
	Very	Moderately	Very
	infrequent	frequent	frequent

Investment	|----------------------------|----------------------------|
	Very	Moderately	Very
	infrequent	frequent	frequent

Authority limits	|----------------------------|----------------------------|
	Very	Moderately	Very
	infrequent	frequent	frequent

Pick one of the tactics that you use very infrequently, a tactic that you feel comfortable adding to your repertoire of negotiating skills. Over the next two days, try to use this tactic as often as you can with as many people as you can. List the uses below. How often was the tactic successful? Why did it fail, if it did? How would you respond if the countermeasure were used on you?

Tactic: _____

Uses: _____

_____

_____

_____

Pick a second tactic (or a countermeasure, if you are not particularly good at one of them) and practice it intensively for two days, monitoring your progress. Then pick a third tactic and do the same. After a week you will have three more tactics to choose from in your future negotiations.

As you practice these tactics, be careful not to reveal the tactic itself—before, during, or after its use—through your glee or excitement. One of the cardinal rules of negotiating is that a tactic revealed is no tactic. Let me illustrate.

Years ago I was in Winnipeg, Canada, with a colleague to do a workshop on conflict management. The night before the workshop, we went out to eat with our host and his three-year-old daughter. With all her curls, she looked like a tiny Shirley Temple. At the restaurant, however, she immediately became agitated and would not sit down. Her father turned to my colleague and me and said, "You are the conflict experts, what do I do?" I knelt down to the three-year-old and asked, "Do you want to sit with me or with your father?" She straightaway chose her father, and sat down quietly. To her father it seemed like magic, but I knew that kids like choices, and I gave her one. Recently, however, I tried the same tactic with a six-year-old who wouldn't leave the school library at the conclusion of an after-school program to return home. I asked if she wanted to leave now or in ten minutes. She turned to me and with a smile said, "We're going to stay all night." Being older, she knew the tactic, and rather than staying within the choices she created her own option.

Once another party knows a tactic, it is more difficult to use it successfully. Most certainly, if you employ a tactic successfully and then reveal it to the other party outright or through a telling smile, you can be sure that your counterpart will react differently to the tactic in the future, if not immediately seek to renegotiate. No one likes to be had.

Many of these tactics involve some form of bluffing. This is certainly true for making an exaggerated first offer, and it is potentially the case for speed-ups, delays, drawing a bottom line, and authority limits. If you use these tactics often enough with the same individuals, you eventually develop a reputation. Sometimes a whole industry develops a reputation, as has the auto sales industry with its rock-bottom first offer on your trade-in (exaggerated first offer) and having to check with the manager (authority limit). Eventually, your reputation precedes you and others presume that everything is a bluff. Perhaps the only thing worse than being caught in a bluff is for the other party to believe that you are bluffing when you are not.

10

More Tactics and Countermeasures

Never cut what you can untie.
                    —Joseph Joubert (1754–1824)

The eight tactics described in Chapter 9 represent common business tactics. There are, of course, many more tactics than just these eight.

More Tactics

Each of the tactics presented in this chapter is worth recognizing, and you might find one or two worth developing. Along with each tactic, one or more countermeasures are offered.

Silence

One of the tactics that I like best is silence. Since information, information, and information, as I suggested previously, constitute the three cornerstones of negotiation, the more you can learn about the other party and his or her needs, the more effective you can be as a negotiator. Silence works particularly well with an opponent who is anxious about a negotiation or who is a natural extravert (thinking out loud).

　　The story is told of a young Thomas Edison who, having invented a stock ticker, was traveling to New York to sell the patent rights to some businessmen. Edison had decided ahead of time that he was going to ask for $5,000 for the invention, but he would settle for $3,000. But when he got to the meeting he was so intimidated by the potential buyers and their trappings that he could hardly speak. After some time had passed, one of the businessmen broke the silence and offered $40,000. Edison was stunned but found his voice in time to accept the offer.

It is hard to believe that if Edison had asked for $5,000 the businessmen would have offered $40,000. Here is a case where involuntary silence works to one's advantage, at least as far as an asking price is concerned. (I wonder what might have transpired if Edison had reacted to the offer with alarm rather than acceptance, or asked for a week to get back to them.)

Sometimes the tactic of silence is best preceded by a statement or open-ended question designed to "bracket" the conversation. The bracket focuses the other party's attention through an image that provokes sensory stimulation: "What do you think about a home with the convenience of the city yet all the natural beauty and tranquillity of the country?" or "What would you say to a six-figure income?" or "*The best* seafood that I have ever tasted." Then silence—one that the other party is likely to fill with information useful to you in the negotiation. (Most commercial ads are a form of bracketing and silence, such as depicting a sexy passenger seated in a new sport utility vehicle.)

An important facet of this tactic in face-to-face negotiations, of course, is listening. You listen with your ears, but you also listen with your eyes. What do the other party's nonverbals tell you about his desire for a six-figure income or a lobster dinner? Do his eyes get big, his lips moist? And if the other party sends a mixed message—denying interest while licking his lips—which sign do you believe? In general, actions (nonverbal actions, in particular) speak louder than words.

Countermeasures: How should you react if someone uses this tactic on you? Obviously, you have to be aware of your nonverbal communication. But you can't simply remain silent. Matching silence with silence may only antagonize your counterpart. The best way to deal with tactical silence, including silence preceded by bracketing, is probably to ask an open-ended question: "Tell me more." The other party wants you to talk, so you talk—but you ask a question, thereby turning the tables. The important point is not to get uncomfortable and give out confidential information. Your goal is to move back into a normal conversational mode in which the other party, not you, offers the information.

Playing Dumb

One of the roles I like to play is that of the neophyte. I learn everything I can about an upcoming negotiation, and then when I go into the negotiation I play dumb. I give that "Huh?" look and let the other party educate me. This tactic seems to work best with repair people, who know a lot more about the refrigerator or the furnace or the car than I do, and who encounter people every day who want to bargain or negotiate with them.

Much like using silence, by playing dumb you can learn more about the furnace (life expectancy, common malfunctions, warranty options), verifying what you already know and checking to see how much the repair person knows. Every once in a while, I like to throw out a piece of knowledge (perhaps in the form of a question) that suggests I am not a moron, a tactic that can catch the person off guard. It raises some doubt in his mind about how knowledgeable I am, and he is less likely to attempt to take advantage of me.

One variation of this tactic sometimes employed in cross-cultural negotiations is using a language interpreter, even if the party understands the language. Using an interpreter often causes the other party to look for multiple ways to say the same thing and gives the party with the interpreter more time to observe and think of a response. In addition, if you really believe the other party cannot understand your language, you may feel more relaxed about sharing tactics or inside information with an associate in the presence of this party (which she, then, hears and knows).

Countermeasures: This is a tough one. If your opponent is skilled in this tactic, you do not really know if he or she needs to be tutored in the values of this product or service, or whether this person is just pulling your leg. On the other hand, if you really know your business, this is an opportunity to establish credibility through a straightforward, matter-of-fact sharing of facts and features.

The problem with sharing this information, even if you steer clear of matters that might weaken your position, is that you do not know how you can help (or hurt) the other party. So look for opportunities to turn the microphone back to the other party, by asking an open-ended question: "Tell me again what you are looking for . . . what you have in mind." This is likely to give you more of the information you need to negotiate effectively.

In terms of cross-cultural negotiations, the other party may be using an interpreter because she is not confident in expressing herself in your language. Nonetheless, you should always assume that she can understand at least some of what you are saying (verbally or nonverbally). Sometimes offering an amusing story or joke can tip you off to the other party's level of understanding. Employing your own interpreter, someone familiar with your counterpart's culture, may provide some additional insights.

Playing the Crazy

When Muhammad Ali (then Cassius Clay) was about to fight Sonny Liston for the first time, few thought Ali stood much of a chance against the powerful champion. Liston feared no one and had won and defended the heavyweight championship with first-round knockouts. At the weigh-in on the day of the fight, Ali began acting like a wild man, shouting and flailing. Some thought he was having a seizure. His pulse shot up to 110 beats per minute, well above the normal 54 beats. He appeared unbalanced, ready to explode. It took six men to hold him down. It was, for all intents and purposes, an act. Ali knew that Liston liked to intimidate his opponents, and the only person who would not be terrified of Liston would be a crazy person. Now Liston thought Ali was crazy.

Getting upset or angry, threatening actions, or acting like a madman are all variations of the same tactic, a tactic that can unnerve an opponent. With this tactic, the other party may be wondering not how you can help but rather how you might hurt him or her. (Remember our Golden Rule?) In a retail setting, the clerk is concerned with the effects this exchange has on other customers. Or a new employee or an employee on probation may be concerned that you will complain to a supervisor.

This tactic can become a quick and easy alternative, particularly for passive-aggressive personalities. For my money, it should be a tactic of last resort. All too frequently, these nasty exchanges come back to haunt you, either through future encounters with the same clerk or through acquiring an unwanted reputation. So think twice before you launch into a hissy fit.

Countermeasures: To deal with this tactic, you must first ascertain whether your opponent is putting on an act or is really deranged. In Muhammad Ali's case, a wink gave him away to one of those present, though not to Sonny Liston.

If the other party is putting on an act, whether you recognize it or not, you can still go about the business of selling your product, service, or idea. Do so by seeking information about the other party's needs or desires: "Tell me more about what you are looking for." The more you learn, the better you can match your product, service, or idea to these needs. You may need to prime the pump first by describing, displaying, or demonstrating something of what you can offer. Showing this person what you know gives you credibility, but it is a shot in the dark unless you know what she needs. So look for opportunities to ask open-ended questions, to learn more about the other party's needs and expectations.

If the other party truly is out of control, calm him through reassurances in an attempt to move to normal behavior and rational discussion. At a minimum, you want to maneuver the other party from a public setting, where his emotional display can negatively affect others (a means of hurting you). If the individual is not only out of control but dangerous, you probably want to avoid the person or withdraw from the situation for safety reasons (this is what some people think Sonny Liston did in his second fight with Muhammad Ali). There really are times to avoid or withdraw, as suggested in Chapter 7, so long as it is a tactic rather than your style or strategy.

Showing Off the Goods

You have probably heard the expression "the product is so good it sells itself." No special marketing or sales gimmicks are needed. They see it, they buy it.

If the product truly is that good, then by all means show it off. Door-to-door salespeople know this, of course. Can you imagine them traveling without an encyclopedia, vacuum cleaner, Tupperware set, or cosmetic kit? Men and women do the same, in a manner of speaking, to attract the attention of potential suitors. We wear clothing that draws attention to us, trying to show off our best features. We wear cologne, perfume, and noisy shoes to signal the olfactory and auditory senses that there is something in the area to check out.

When I was a graduate student, I was interested in doing some consulting for fun and profit. Being young (and looking younger), I knew that first impressions might be difficult to overcome. After all, would you turn your organization over to a baby-faced unknown? As a student, however, I had taken a course in consulting in which we had to complete an organizational climate analysis with a local company. The report I wrote was well written and useful, at least according to the feedback I had received. So when I went to look for professional (paying) consulting opportunities, I brought along a copy of my report. "Here, this is an example of what I can do." I approached two organizations and got two jobs.

Some negotiators take showing off the goods one step further. Not only do you get a chance to see the final product and try it out, but you get to keep it for thirty days. America Online sends out free software and allows you so many hours of free access to the Internet. Similar introductory offers are made in television ads for books, records, household gadgets, and much more. If you are not completely satisfied, you can return it for a full refund, cancel your subscription, or buy more books, records, etc., in the series. Statistics show that only 10–20 percent of those initial offers are ever returned.

Countermeasures: In truth, you want to see the goods. You

don't want to buy from a catalog, if you can help it. Nor do you want to buy something shown under artificial conditions. Automobiles displayed in a climate-controlled showroom, clean and waxed with spotlights strategically positioned, can be dazzling. If possible, you want to test it under everyday conditions, and then learn as much as you can about the specifications, guarantees, and warranties. You want to know if you will really use that treadmill or ab conditioner, especially after the novelty wears off.

But you must also have the ability to cancel or return the original merchandise, and withstand subsequent offers that might come from having given out your name and address. If you tend to procrastinate on such things, or have difficulty saying no, you might enlist a spouse or friend (authority limit) to assist you. Placing a phone call and asking that no further advertisements be sent is likely to put a stop to follow-up calls.

Flattery

As was suggested in Chapter 7 on negotiation styles, creating a sense of relationship (friendship) often prompts the other party to reveal information, concede issues, and forgive transgressions. This can be done by using familial language (for example, first names), speaking in softer tones, and sitting close to the other person.

Beyond establishing a "friendship," negotiators sometimes encourage, congratulate, and flatter the other party as a way of playing on ego. "Oh, that coat looks divine on you. You've got to have it." "We wanted to go with the best advertising firm in the business, and that's you." "I love that sweater. Where did you get it?" I met a real estate broker once who would take pictures of his clients and send copies of the photos to them. This works because we all have egos, and because in many cases we are capable of meeting the terms desired by the other party; we would prefer to think that we got a deal. Most retail stores build this right into the sale, maintaining many (if not most) of their goods continuously on sale.

Flattery can also focus on the process of negotiation. I once observed in a classroom negotiation, for example, a student with considerable sales experience flatter his opponent by telling her what a great job she was doing in the multi-issue negotiation. He was very believable. But when the final results were tallied, he had clearly gotten the better of her. And guess what: She didn't seem to care.

To be effective, the flattery must be believable. Not everyone can carry this off, but some negotiators are superb at it.

Countermeasures: If your counterpart is really good at this tactic, it may be difficult to detect his or her insincerity. One thing to be cognizant of is the opportunity for a long-term relationship in this negotiating situation. If you are buying a used boat from another party, for example, unless you already know this party or are neighbors you are not likely to ever see him again. If you are having a moving sale, you probably won't see the other party again. By examining the context of the negotiation, you may be able to recognize the inappropriateness of flattery.

In response, you can politely acknowledge the comments with a thank-you and change the tenor of the interaction and focus of the conversation by returning to the open-ended question tactic ("Thanks, tell me about your business"). Be careful to avoid returning the flattery in a manner that suggests you are calling the person on her faint praise, as this can create ill-feeling. No one likes to have tactics revealed or reciprocated.

Buying Your Objections

It is Friday afternoon and you are just getting ready to leave work. Two coworkers, John and Martha, stop by to say that they are going out to a quiet bar-restaurant for a drink and perhaps a bite to eat. They want you to join them.

You: I'd like to, but I don't have my car.
Martha: No problem. I'm driving and I'll bring you back here or take you home afterward.
You: Well, I really need to stop by Regal Dry Cleaners to pick up some slacks.
John: We can stop by there on the way to the restaurant.

You: Yes, but I have to catch an early morning flight to Boston tomorrow.

Martha: We'll only be out for an hour or two. And I can take you to the airport tomorrow if you need a ride.

Buying another party's objections is a tactic for dealing with the multiplicity of needs and desires that sometimes stand in the way of an agreement. Of all the tactics that we have discussed and will discuss, this is probably one of the most benign. It can be a means of sorting through the many answers to the fundamental question "What do I want?" (some of which may be buried in our subconscious) as well as a way of moving from positions to interests. In this respect, buying your objections can be a useful tactic for both parties.

Here is an illustration. Several years ago Waste Management was trying to lure Ronald T. LeMay, the number-two executive at Sprint into becoming the new chief executive officer. The company offered him a $2.5 million salary, plus options on four million shares of stock. He declined, concerned that he would lose the future gains on his Sprint options. So Waste Management offered to give him up to one million shares of Sprint stock as part of the contract. Ultimately, LeMay accepted the offer.

There is at least one other variation of this tactic, an approach that can be used at the end of a negotiation as effectively as near the beginning. Rather than waiting for your objections, the other party asks you straight off "What will it take to get you to join us?" or "What will it take to close this deal at $60,000?" The what-will-it-take question cuts right to your needs and concerns, moving from positions to interests.

Countermeasures: There may be circumstances under which you do not want the other party to buy you out of your objections. It could be that the real reason you don't want to go out with colleagues after work is because you are embarrassed about your plans for the evening (for example, to watch a rerun of an old television show). Much like physicians prescribing medication in gradually stronger dosages, many of us put up an initial objection that we hope is sufficient without creating side effects. If this doesn't work, we gradually increase the strength of our objections ("I need to be ready for my early morning flight and meeting.").

If the offer is one that you truly wish to refuse, you are going to have to present a much more substantial objection or a counterproposal (maybe a rain check on this particular happy hour). Generally, if you express appreciation or gratitude for the invitation and wrap your reasoning for turning down the offer in nonverbal language consistent with your resolve, you will put an end to the buying of objections.

Lowballing

Lowballing is a tactic that you are most likely to encounter in a retail setting, particularly for big-ticket items. It generally occurs when the other party (seller) recognizes that you are intent on shopping around and have just begun your journey. Before you leave, the salesperson suggests that she might be able to get you the item that you are interested in for under $5,000. You do not know it at the time, but it is impossible to find this item for under $5,000. After shopping around all weekend, you finally realize that the first store had the best price. But when you get there, you discover that they won't sell you the item for under $5,000 either. Any number of excuses are offered: that salesperson is not working today, it was a one-day offer, there was a miscalculation, the boss won't go along with it. Tired, you end up paying the asking price, something higher, just to be done with the process.

Countermeasures: The more information you have before you go into a negotiation, the better off you are. If the salesperson's offer sounds sweet, ask him to put the offer in writing. Be careful not to put down a deposit, however, which he may request, since this binds you psychologically to the sale (the investment tactic).

If you get trapped by a lowball tactic, having shopped all weekend and now you are ready to go back to the first place that made you the phenomenal offer, your best option is probably to walk away and restart your search and purchase next weekend. Chances are that a lowballing tactic is only the tip of the iceberg with this retail operation, and you probably cannot count on much service or support if something should go wrong with the product.

Strawman

This tactic is a variation on the concessions tactic, but in this case what you are conceding is something of little or no value to you. But don't tell the other party this; instead, use the supposed concession to gain something of value.

Suppose that while in the process of negotiating the sale of your house, the other party insists that you throw in the washer and dryer. You have no need for them, because you are already planning to purchase a new washer and dryer for your new home. In fact, the thought of having to sell or dispose of these two appliances is just one more thing that you dread having to take care of. Rather than respond to the buyer's demand with relief ("Sure, they're yours"), which is one legitimate approach, you hesitate: "Hmmm. I don't know." In so doing, you create the perception that these items have value for you where, in fact, little or none exists. In return, you can ask for something from the buyer immediately: "Okay, I'll throw in the washer and dryer, but then you have to take care of repairing the leak in the garage roof." Or you can hold on to the advantage until you encounter a sticking point later in the negotiation against which this seeming concession can be played. The issue or concession appears to the other party to be valuable to you, but in fact it is without substance; it is a strawman.

The delay tactic can be used as a strawman as well. Parties delay because they are uncertain about a transaction and want to get more information, or perhaps sleep on it. They also delay to see the other party's reaction. How anxious is the other party to settle? If a delay is not necessary (that is, only a ploy), then it can be traded against something of value by the party declaring the need to "get back to you next week." Since it is human nature to want the other party to offer one or more concessions, some negotiators create the illusion of a concession to satisfy the need.

Countermeasures: This can be a difficult tactic to counter if the other party is effective in distorting the value of an issue or item, since you can't counter what you can't detect. The best approach is never to get into this situation in the first place by making offers. It is better if the offers or trial agreements come from the other party. After all, they need you more than you need them. So ask open-ended questions to learn their needs, which puts you in a position to use the strawman tactic.

Another approach, if you have already gotten yourself into a position where the strawman can be used against you, is to create a sense of future relationship. As a buyer, discuss your intentions of purchasing more product or service in the future, as your organization grows. Few negotiators want their opponents to catch them in a lie or bluff. The more opportunities there are for future contact (business or friendship), the greater the possibility that the strawman will be revealed for what it is, and the party who created it revealed as well. This potential for loss of face and destruction of trust may be enough to deter the other party from using the tactic.

Finally, if you suspect that you have fallen into this situation, you can always try bluffing: "Well, that's not so critical. Never mind." This is most effective if you have a BATNA.

Bundling

Not so different from the strawman is a technique called bundling. This involves wrapping together two or more issues or items of mixed value, hoping that the value of one is sufficient to cover the cost of the other. Bundling occurs in many different settings, including (and especially) public policy and budget negotiations.

When the president of the United States, together with members of his party, puts together a welfare reform package or creates a new transportation policy or proposes funding for new defense projects, invariably other members of Congress add amendments and riders to the initiative that on their own would not earn the necessary support of the president and Congress, but relative to the larger initiative are tolerated in order to gain passage.

Bundling can occur at any point throughout a negotiation, including the end. At this last point, it is sometimes referred to as "one for the road." The other party has finally exhaled, believing that an agreement is now at hand. She has, in effect, made an emotional commitment to signing the papers, exchanging money for machinery, etc. Then, you say, more as a summative statement than a question, "You will cover the delivery expenses." Having come this far, the other party is likely to acquiesce. You have just bundled one final request with the preceding negotiated package. For many retail tire stores, one for the road is simply part of everyday business. The price for a set of four new radials for your car, as advertised in today's newspaper, looks like an incredible deal. But when you get to the store (or when you get the final bill, if you don't ask up front) you discover that valve stems and balancing are extra. Plus, there is a charge for disposing of your old tires! Ultimately, it costs you 50 percent more than the advertised price for the tires, but by now you are so committed to getting this taken care of that you approve the work anyway.*

Countermeasures: To avoid disadvantageous bundling early in a negotiation, be sure you know what you want. (Remember the first fundamental question of negotiation.) This means not just the issue that is most important to you, but the value of all the issues.

To avoid becoming one-for-the-roadkill at the conclusion of a negotiation, make sure that all the issues have been put on the table ("Do you have any other items you want to discuss?"), and then summarize. You might begin by labeling your summative behavior ("Can I summarize the issues?") before listing and clarifying the issues with the other party. Put them in writing (legal pad, flip chart) for everyone to see. Then negotiate the final package.

Confederates

The adage that there is strength in numbers applies to negotiating as well as to lifting a barge or toting a bale. When four people

---

*One for the road is not to be confused with reacting to the winner's curse. This is a state of mind that often follows winning, particularly in a negotiation. Suddenly you wonder if maybe this came too easily. Perhaps you could have gotten more for less. Seeking to reopen negotiations because of the winner's curse is different from a tactical maneuver like one for the road, and a behavior that should be avoided.

show up for a contract negotiation, it says that this is a matter of importance to more than just a single individual. This group took the time and associated risks to attend the meeting. It says something. Edison was intimidated by the potential buyers of his stock ticker in part because of their trappings, but also because of their number and their collective experience.

You may be thinking, How many people are enough? Two? Five? Ten? The answer is: more than the other party is expecting. A good deal of tactical negotiating has to do with putting the opposition in an unfamiliar position. Just like basketball players attempting to defend a star opponent by making him or her take unusual or unfamiliar shots, you can influence a negotiating opponent's pattern by bringing allies when she is accustomed to negotiating one-on-one. Your associates need not say much of anything, and perhaps should not say much, but it causes your counterpart to wonder what they will say—whom to address, with whom to make eye contact—and think twice about pulling any fast ones.

Countermeasures: The best things in life are not free, but unexpected. Unfortunately, so are the worst things. Generally speaking, you do not want to be surprised to find four people in your office. So whenever possible, find out ahead of time how many to expect. You can always invite associates of your own.

If you are taken by surprise, keep in mind that your goal for this meeting does not have to be forging an agreement (although this may be your counterpart's intent). Rather, take control of the meeting, refocus the agenda on fact-finding, be accommodating to your guests, learn everything you can, and then arrange for another meeting (so you have more time to plan and prepare on your terms).

Good Guy, Bad Guy

Good guy, bad guy (sometimes called good cop, bad cop) is a tactic used by a negotiating pair (a husband and wife, two friends or roommates, business partners). It contains elements of two prior tactics—confederates and authority limits—but differs in that it creates a false sense of alliance between one member of the pair and their opponent.

You and your wife go into a furniture store to buy a new sofa for your family room. There is a particular sofa that you really like, unbeknownst to the salesman. "It's a beautiful sofa, isn't it?" he says, noticing that you have paused at this model. "Yes, it is very nice," you say. You sit down on it. "It's very comfortable. What do you think, honey?" Your wife does not appear as enthralled. "Does it come in any other colors?" she asks. There is an assortment of fabrics and colors from which to choose. "I am not sure I like the arms on it," she says, speaking to you but loud enough that the salesman can overhear. "I think they are similar to those on our recliner," you reply. "I don't know," she says, lifting up the price tag, then walking around to the back of the sofa.

The salesman excuses himself and then returns shortly. You and your wife are still discussing the sofa. "We are still looking," you say as he approaches. Then your wife drifts off to other pieces of furniture. "I think she might go for it with a different fabric and if it wasn't quite so expensive," you say to the salesman. Now it appears to the salesman that he has sold you and only needs to sell your wife on the sofa, and that you will help. In fact, you appear to be *asking* for his help. You want the sofa. You are on his side. You are the "good guy" and your wife is the "bad guy," but she is the boss (authority limit). So you act as a go-between or mediator, when in fact you are not at all neutral.

This negotiation depicts a "good" bad guy (that is, a relatively mild-mannered bad guy). There are, of course, bad bad guys, who are angry, combative, and explosive. In the case of a bad bad guy, the good guy becomes twice as valuable to the salesman because this pair not only can help the store through a sale but can also hurt the store through loss of customers, depending on how deranged the bad guy becomes.

The good-guy, bad-guy tactic is sometimes employed with the bad guy physically absent from the negotiation. In a business negotiation with a potential supplier, for example, you are anxious to close the deal. However, the engineering department is not that keen on the supplier's product. As the good guy, you negotiate "cooperatively" with the supplier, seeking to appease the engineering department through trade-offs and concessions.*

Countermeasures: The best response to this tactic, if it truly is a tactic and not a case of one person liking an item and the other person (or department) not liking it, is to create some competition for your time and for the item. If you are the salesperson and there are other customers in the furniture store, excuse yourself momentarily to attend to them. If these other customers are interested in sofas, bring them over to see this one. Is this the last model of this type in the store? If the good guy and the bad guy are at all motivated buyers, you should see a reaction.

In a situation where key stakeholders to the negotiation are absent (someone from engineering, for example), you may be better off proposing that another meeting be set to include those individuals. The other party is likely to quickly forget about the engineers' concerns if this is simply a tactic.

Split the Difference

This tactic is used most frequently during bargaining when two parties appear to have communicated implicitly that each wants an agreement, but even after each has made concessions they are still apart on a final settlement. At this stage, the gap is likely small, and rather than one side capitulating, it is suggested that they split the difference. That is, if we are stuck between your offer of $15,000 and my desire for $15,500, we could split the difference between our two positions (half of $500) and settle at $15,250. This is a tactic for closing out a negotiation in which you have gotten most of what you want, and if you began at an exaggerated initial offer, splitting the difference may still put you well ahead of where you want to finally settle.

*Another variation of the one-person good guy, bad guy occurs when a customer attempting to return or exchange an item in a retail store becomes irate and is rebuffed by the store representative. As this customer storms off, you approach the representative with your request. Happy to see a sane customer and prove that he is not unreasonable, the store representative might make accommodations for you that would be turned down under normal circumstances. In this case, you are playing off the prior customer's unwitting bad-guy role.

Splitting the difference can occur with a final price, but it can also apply to the quantity (for example, a ten-voice chorus or a twenty-voice chorus) and the time (meet at one o'clock versus two o'clock).

Countermeasures: Usually, this tactic is something that both sides can readily accept, since it often comes near the end of a negotiation, when both parties are ready to conclude. If the final settlement price is an issue that is very important for you, starting at a much higher (or lower) amount is one countermeasure. You can also bundle this compromise with another issue: "Okay, I will agree to split the difference if you will provide free delivery." If the negotiation has "concluded" (that is, the other party has relaxed and is ready to shake hands, make the exchange, or sign a contract), this tactic is more appropriately called *one for the road*.

Generally speaking, you are better off if it's the other party who makes the offer to split the difference. Then, when you reluctantly accept, the other party feels that he has won. Alternatively, you can respond with a counteroffer to the other party's proposed split that brings the final settlement closer to your original offer (for example, you propose $15,200).

Combination Tactics

It is also possible, of course, to encounter (and use) combinations of these tactics. The good guy (good-guy, bad-guy tactic) tries to get the salesperson to invest more and more time in explaining the features and values of a product (investment tactic), in part to convince the bad guy. Flattery is combined with playing dumb ("You sure have some nice things. What's this one? . . . How does it work?").

A friend was applying to colleges and universities. There were two schools that she was most interested in, one in her home town and the other several hundred miles away, comparable in every respect and both excellent universities. She received notification from the out-of-town school that she had been accepted and would receive a full-tuition scholarship. However, as time passed, she was up against a deadline to let them know whether she would be attending. She had not yet heard from the local university, which technically would not send out notifications for another week. She called this school on a Friday and said: "I have been admitted to XYZ University on a full-tuition scholarship. I have to let them know next week." Monday she received a letter from the local university accepting her and offering a full-tuition scholarship. She thus combined the creating-competition and speed-ups tactics, with perhaps a dash of drawing the line thrown in.

As this negotiation suggests, combining two or more tactics can bring added pressure to the other party to make an offer or concession. Sometimes the use of multiple tactics is really a smoke screen, because one tactic is being employed to disguise another. For example, flattery and making concessions are a means of disguising an exaggerated initial offer.

Before we make this too complicated, let's go back and review each of these additional tactics. How frequently do you think you use each of them? Indicate your comfort and frequency of use by placing an *X* on the scales shown below.

Tactic	*Use*		
Silence	Very infrequent	Moderately frequent	Very frequent
Playing dumb	Very infrequent	Moderately frequent	Very frequent
Playing the crazy	Very infrequent	Moderately frequent	Very frequent
Showing off the goods	Very infrequent	Moderately frequent	Very frequent
Flattery	Very infrequent	Moderately frequent	Very frequent

Tactic	*Use*		
Buying your objections	Very infrequent	Moderately frequent	Very frequent
Lowballing	Very infrequent	Moderately frequent	Very frequent
Strawman	Very infrequent	Moderately frequent	Very frequent
Bundling	Very infrequent	Moderately frequent	Very frequent
Confederates	Very infrequent	Moderately frequent	Very frequent
Good guy, bad guy	Very infrequent	Moderately frequent	Very frequent
Split the difference	Very infrequent	Moderately frequent	Very frequent

You might find it worthwhile selecting one or two of the tactics that are particularly appealing, but that you have not yet mastered, to practice over the next couple of days. The larger your repertoire of tactics, the more effective you are as a negotiator. Once again, consider a full range of social and business settings (for example, retail stores) as venues for practicing these tactics. The more you practice, the more natural these tactics become for you.

11

Measuring Your Skill With Countermeasures

A Salary Negotiation

Only the wearer knows where the shoe pinches.
—English proverb

You now have four or five additional tactics that you feel more confident in using. These are, of course, tactics you can decide to use (or not use) as you see fit. This choice is determined by a variety of factors—your relationship to the other party, the issues, the stakes—not to mention your ethics. More on ethics and negotiation shortly.

The opportunities to practice new tactics are probably far more plentiful than the opportunities to practice countermeasures to these tactics. You are dependent upon other parties initiating a tactic before you have any chance of practicing your response to it. Some tactics come around so infrequently that you can be taken by surprise and miss out altogether. At other times, you are so emotionally wrapped up in the negotiation that you may not perceive the opportunity.

It is at least as useful to master countermeasures as the tactics themselves; they are a means of taking control of a negotiation by redirecting your counterpart's energy and focus (a form of mental or social jujitsu, if you will). Although some individuals may hold to standards that limit their psychological comfort in using certain tactics, few would deny you your right to defend yourself.

A Negotiation to Practice Countermeasures

Given the importance of countermeasures and the scarcity of opportunities to practice them, here is a negotiation offered as a vehicle for sharpening your skills. For this negotiation, you again need a single negotiating partner. In this case, it might be better if your counterpart is someone with whom you have already negotiated (for example, the person who represented Continental Glass in the Valero Wine–Continental Glass negotiation in Chapter 6); he or she would already understand the process to be followed in such a negotiation. However, if you want to ask a different person to work with you, that's fine also.

This negotiation involves a job performance review and request for a salary adjustment at a publishing company called Carson Enterprises. You are a sales employee at Carson, and your counterpart is your manager. As with the Valero Wine–Continental Glass negotiation, each negotiator has his or her confidential information. Once again, the amount of time allotted for this negotiation is fifteen to twenty minutes.

Listed below are the twenty tactics that were covered in the two preceding chapters. Which of these tactics do you have the most difficulty responding to? Put a check mark in front of at least five but no more than ten of these tactics. (Note: some tactics are difficult for the other party to employ without an ally or a prop and therefore can be left out of this negotiation: showing off the goods; confederates; and good guy, bad guy. Thus they are shown in parentheses.) During the course of the next negotiation, your negotiating counterpart is going to pick at least two or three of the tactics that you have checked to use at some point during your negotiation. This gives you an opportunity to practice your countermeasures in a controlled situation.

___ 1. Exaggerated first offer	___ 11. Playing the crazy
___ 2. Speed-ups	___(12. Showing off the goods)
___ 3. Delays	___ 13. Flattery
___ 4. Drawing lines	___ 14. Buying your objections
___ 5. Creating competition	___ 15. Lowballing
___ 6. Concessions	___ 16. Strawman
___ 7. Investment	___ 17. Bundling
___ 8. Authority limits	___(18. Confederates)
___ 9. Silence	___(19. Good guy, bad guy)
___10. Playing dumb	___ 20. Split the difference

After you have selected the tactics to which you want to practice responding, share them with the other party. Ask your partner to check these off on his or her list, shown in Appendix B, "Sales Manager, Carson Enterprises (Confidential Facts)." The appendix list has some specific directives for your counterpart, so don't look at it yourself.

Once this is complete, you may want to go back and review each of the tactics that you checked, and how to deal with them. That is, review the countermeasures suggested in the previous chapters. Keep in mind that your negotiating partner may or may not choose to employ a specific tactic. Before you begin negotiating, remind yourself of the three fundamental questions of negotiation, and some of the behaviors of successful negotiators that were discussed in Chapter 5. Your confidential information follows.

SALESPERSON, CARSON ENTERPRISES
(Confidential Facts)

You work in the sales division of a publishing company called Carson Enterprises, whose primary product is a monthly magazine. You joined the company eight months ago with some experience in sales. At the time of your employment, the marketplace was very tight for sales jobs (although there seem to be more job openings now). You have your own client base at Carson Enterprises, which has been fairly receptive to placing ads in your magazine. You are generally happy with your job.

When you were hired, there was some mention of a six-month performance review. Assuming a positive review, you will receive either a higher base salary, a higher commission rate, or both.

Your current base salary is $40,000, and your current commission rate is 2 percent on all sales greater than $1 million. So far, you have brought in about $800,000. However, there has been no formal six-month review, and nothing has been scheduled or mentioned by your supervisor, the head of sales. You would like a performance review and the benefits that come from a positive evaluation. Therefore, you have asked to talk with the sales manager, your boss.

Proceed with the negotiation.

Evaluating the Negotiation

Do you have a negotiated agreement? How well do you think you did in this negotiation? Indicate your sense of the outcome by circling a number on the scale below.

You

| 1 | 2 | 3 | 4 | 5 | 6 | 7 |

Not well   Very well

How well do you think the other party (your boss) did? Indicate how well, circling a number on the scale below.

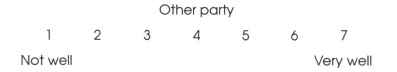

Other party

| 1 | 2 | 3 | 4 | 5 | 6 | 7 |

Not well   Very well

What do you think you did well in this negotiation, particularly regarding how you countered the sales director's use of certain tactics? Record these thoughts in the following box.

1. _____

2. _____

3. _____

4. _____

5. _____

What do you think you did not do so well, and what would you do differently next time? Be as specific as you can.

1. _____

2. _____

3. _____

4. _____

5. _____

If you haven't done so already, exchange confidential information with your negotiating counterpart to see the conditions under which each of you was negotiating. Ask your counterpart which of the tactics he or she employed during the course of the negotiation. Share your perceptions of what you think you did well and what you feel you still need to work on. Ask for feedback from your counterpart as to what he or she thought you did well and what you need to continue to work on.

You might have discerned from the previous two chapters that many countermeasures involve pursuing (or avoiding) one or more of the eight behaviors of successful negotiators presented in Chapter 5. These behaviors are useful in subtly and indirectly changing the mood or focus created by a tactic. If you have difficulty remembering the various countermeasures, or you find yourself overwhelmed or confused in a negotiation, just ask open-ended questions. This behavior works as a countermeasure in many situations, and it buys you time to gather your wits as well as gives you additional information.

You might want more practice using countermeasures. This negotiation is robust enough that it can be repeated, preferably with another individual playing the role of the sales manager but, in a pinch, with the same person. You can pick a new set of tactics for the sales manager to incorporate into his or her role. You can even ask a third party to change some of the key numerical data in the respective roles, to provide another level of uncertainty. These data are the underlined numbers in the Confidential Information sections for the salesperson (given previously) and sales manager at Carson Enterprises (in Appendix B).

Your counterpart may have chosen to play the role of a tough negotiator in the simulation. You have undoubtedly encountered such people from time to time. How do you deal with someone who is a tough negotiator? Are all tough negotiators the same? The next chapter offers some suggestions for spotting and dealing with three types of tough negotiators.

12

Dealing With Tough Negotiators

We boil at different degrees.

—Ralph Waldo Emerson

We have all encountered individuals with whom it is difficult to negotiate. In fact, if you accept my broad definition of negotiation given in Chapter 1, I'd say we have all encountered individuals who are difficult, period.

Three Types of Tough Negotiator

With regard to tough negotiators, I have concluded that there are three types of individuals who fall into this category (Table 12-1). One type is the genuine article, the hard-core toughie. This type likes to win, needs to win, and will win. They are battlers. They are stubborn. They do not give in. It is their way or the highway. How they got to be this tough one can only speculate, but they are your worst nightmare. In terms of tactics, they set extreme bargaining positions. Then, they maintain their positions or make concessions grudgingly. They ignore deadlines. They make up their own rules. Any "kindness" on their part is merely a front. In the worst cases, you have to lose for them to believe that they have won. They are pathologic. Included in this group is Catbert, the evil HR director from Scott Adams's cartoon

Table 12-1: Three Types of Tough Negotiators

Type	Style	Examples
Hard-core toughie	Aggressive-aggressive	Catbert Cruella de Vil James Bond villains Mafiosi
Provoked toughie	Passive-aggressive	Schroeder Frasier Crane Jamie Buchman Clark Kent (Superman) Popeye
Faux toughie	Aggressive-passive	Lou Grant and Ted Baxter Major Margaret Houlihan Hagar the Horrible The Cowardly Lion

strip Dilbert; Cruella de Vil (from the film *101 Dalmatians*); most of the James Bond villains; and the Mafia.

A second type of tough negotiator is the provoked toughie. This type is able and willing to move past positions to explore interests and options. Unlike the hard-core toughie, whose sense of self is synonymous with winning, the provoked toughie does not live or die by the outcome and certainly does not need to see you lose to be satisfied with the outcome. However, the provoked toughie operates by a set of principles that, if attacked or threatened, cause him to hold his ground (like the consulting friend in Chapter 9 who refused to leave the office of a client company until it paid her for services rendered). They are the passive-aggressives of negotiation. Included in this group are Schroeder, the piano-playing Beethoven devotee from the Peanuts comic strip (particularly when he is provoked by Lucy); Frasier Crane, from the sitcom "Frasier" (particularly when he is provoked by Bulldog); Jamie Buchman, from the television show "Mad About You"; Clark Kent (a.k.a. Superman); and Popeye (who, when finally pushed to his limit, declares "Tha's all I can stands, I can't stands no more").

Finally, there is the faux toughie. This is the individual who appears gruff and hard on the outside but who is as soft as angel's hair on the inside. In some cases they are, at their core, almost childlike (silly, playful, anxious to please). Knowing that they have an inner soft spot, these individuals have convinced themselves that they need to put up a façade to protect themselves. They are Lou Grant and Ted Baxter from "The Mary Tyler Moore Show," Major Margaret Houlihan ("Hot Lips") from the film and TV show *M*A*S*H*, Hagar the Horrible from the comic strip by the same name, and the Cowardly Lion in *The Wizard of Oz*. Arithmetically, the more huff and puff they produce, the softer they truly are on the inside, in my experience. They are the aggressive-passives of negotiation.

Let's deal with these three types in reverse order.

The Faux Toughie

This person is crying out for friendship but is afraid of losing control. He is afraid of being found out, of losing respect or being taken advantage of. In the case of males (including Cowardly Lions), the gruff exterior may be as much a perceived social expectation as anything: men are strong, tough, macho. In the case of "Hot Lips" Houlihan, she is the 4077th's sole female officer in a man's army. She undoubtedly feels the need to project competence, respect, resolve, and grit. And she does, at least in her most public moments.

The only real danger in dealing with the faux toughie is in not recognizing her for what she is, and presuming that this person is a hard-core toughie and avoiding her. Unlike the provoked toughie, who shows a more accommodating or collaborating side first, the faux toughie (like the hard-core toughie) often first shows a commanding or competitive side. Therefore, based on first impressions, it is easy to mistake the faux toughie for the hard-core toughie.

In negotiating with the faux toughie, there are really two negotiations. The first involves negotiating his public identity. Recognize what the faux toughie wants (respect) and give it to him. Use titles (Mister, Major, King of the Jungle) and give him physical space. Unless respect is what you also want, it costs you little or nothing. You may even want to show a little toughness (competitiveness) yourself, and then back off, as a way of affirming the other party's desired public identity. Generally, faux toughies like this give-and-take. Then, by lowering your voice (perhaps to the level of a private conversation) and explaining the situation and your needs (which may also be the faux toughie's needs), you are likely to get what you want. This is the second negotiation, which is substantive rather than psychological.

But don't make the mistake of trying to change the faux toughie's public identity in a single negotiation. In all likelihood, it cannot be done (the Cowardly Lion excepted). Any threat to his public image could be met with additional toughness, culminating in a loud and abrupt end to the negotiation. Over the longer term of a relationship and in private, however, you are likely to find that the faux toughie lets down his guard.

The Provoked Toughie

The provoked toughie, as the adjective suggests, is aroused by situational factors. It could be that this person has just had a bad day, and something pushes her past the threshold of accommodative or collaborative behavior. This is not uncommon in parents, who, after a long day (and night), finally get pushed to their limit by the kids and "blow their stack." In a very real sense, most of us fit into this category of toughies. We all have a tolerance level, a threshold, although some of us are more quickly provoked than others. This type of toughie also can become aggressive when personally held principles are threatened or breached (for example, when Lucy demeans the reputation of Beethoven, Schroeder pulls the piano out from under her).

The implicit communication of the provoked toughie is, "If you keep away from the behaviors or issues that bother me, everything will be all right. That is, I can hurt you by being aggressive—by not being your friend—so avoid the things that might set me off." Thus, the way to deal with the provoked toughie is to avoid, if possible, those things that might provoke her, or if she has already been provoked, to address her immediate concerns. If timing and energy are the concerns (a bad day at the office, the kids are driving me nuts, I've got a ton of work to do today), negotiate another day or time that is better for all parties to focus on the substantive issues. If personally held principles are the concern (for example, work comes before play), address those up front. It is only after the provoked toughie's immediate concerns have been dealt with that she is able to address your immediate concerns.

The Hard-Core Toughie

This type of toughie is frustrating, and in some cases dangerous. Often they are hard to detect, since their modus operandi varies. By giving the appearance that they are friendly and supportive, for example, the hard-core toughie can lure you into letting down your guard and revealing important information about your style or position. By overwhelming you initially with assertiveness or aggression, they test your limits and establish their dominance. Once you have been measured, they can afford to appear passive and cooperative as they pursue their ends. Learning all you can about the style and reputation of a negotiating counterpart prior to engaging an individual is always a good idea in an important negotiation, but particularly if the individual is a toughie. You also can tell a lot about an individual by sizing up friends and foes. Are the friends people whose integrity and consideration for others you admire? How about the foes? What is their reputation?

If you choose to negotiate with a known hard-core toughie, consider first negotiating the process whereby you are to negotiate. Insist on fair principles, uninterrupted statements, active listening, and no abusive language or shouting. By using some of the behaviors described in Chapter 5 (asking questions, testing understanding and summarizing, giving internal information, explaining before disagreeing), you model the type of behavior you want the hard-core toughie to employ.

Many hard-core toughies, however, are not good at responding to (let alone using) such behaviors. Therefore, do not be surprised if a hard-core toughie tries to change the tenor of a negotiation through accusations, outbursts, threats, etc., particularly if he is not getting his way. Refuse to become a victim, and don't fall into the trap of trying to beat the hard-core toughie at his own game. He expects you to cave in to his antics and demands, or to become defensive, resist, and counterattack. Rather than play to his strength, ignore his behavior and ask open-ended questions, listen, summarize, and point out areas of common interest, all the while staying focused on what you want. Try to think as a third-party mediator, searching for the other party's needs and interests (among which is to maintain his pride and honor). How can you help or hurt him? Seek ways to help the hard-core toughie feel safer, and statements or proposals to which he can say yes. If the outbursts and abuse continue despite your attempts to ignore or redirect them, reassert the principles under which you will continue negotiating, and the potential consequences of terminating discussions.

Occasionally you encounter a truly hard-core toughie with whom these behaviors have little or no apparent effect, someone only interested in his self-interest and winning—generally at the expense of others. Even if you think that you have finally reached an agreement with such an individual, you are likely to discover that he interprets the terms differently, or that the agreement will not be honored in whole or in part. Negotiating with these hard-core toughies feels like war, and there are no rules in war. In all likelihood, you will only negotiate with a truly hard-core toughie if you do not have a BATNA, or if your own personality or style fits with his style (dominant-submissive). Don't get beat up physically, socially, psychologically, or financially if you don't have to. This is the time to choose not to negotiate (as described in Chapter 1) and exercise your BATNA.

Unfortunately, there may be circumstances where you feel that avoiding or withdrawing is not possible because you are socially bound to a hard-core toughie. If this person is your direct supervisor (and you need the job) or a relative (father, daughter, husband, wife), you may not have a quick and easy alternative to withdrawing from him or her. In such cases, negotiation is sure to require greater influence or pressure than you alone can exert. Affected family members of an alcoholic and abusive parent, for example, have been known to effectively confront the individual en masse in an effort to communicate the seriousness of the behavior and get the individual to go into a special treatment program. Countries seek sanctions and support from the United

Nations as a means of communicating the seriousness of an aggressor nation's behavior in the hope that this behavior can be altered. Such was the case in 1991 when United Nations forces took joint action against Iraq following that country's invasion of Kuwait. There is strength in numbers.

Keep in mind, however, that changing someone's style is a long shot, and the few truly hard-core toughies to experience an epiphany were for the most part fictional characters (like Ebenezer Scrooge from Charles Dickens's *A Christmas Carol*). If it is not the case that you are bound to this individual by blood or something thicker, look for one or more BATNAs to give you some flexibility.

13

Written Agreements

A verbal contract isn't worth the paper it's written on.
—Samuel Goldwyn

Earlier in this book you completed a negotiation involving gift-sized wine bottles. At the conclusion of the negotiation you were asked to record the terms of your agreement. Although most everyday nonbusiness negotiations are completed with a handshake or less, many business negotiations require putting things in writing.

There are a number of reasons for doing so, but perhaps the most important is to make sure that everyone is clear on what will occur and when it will occur. Many times it is not ill intention but rather miscommunication that foils implementing an agreement. We have all heard, if not experienced firsthand, sad yet hilarious stories in which each party thought the other was picking up Mom (or Cathy, or Junior) and everyone arrived at their destination except Mom, or Cathy, or Junior.

This type of misunderstanding occurs in business and government as well. An administrator at a major university hospital where I was working once asked me to attend a departmental meeting. Upon arrival, I discovered to my surprise that the sole purpose of the meeting was to discuss a report I had written. This wasn't a ploy or a tactic. No one was out to embarrass me. Rather, no one had taken the time or remembered to tell me the reason for the meeting, and there was no written announcement or agenda.*

*For an amusing illustration of what happens in meetings if agreements are not recorded, see John Cleese in the classic video "Meetings, Bloody Meetings." The dream sequence in which Cleese plays a bailiff who decides to try to remember everyone's sentence, rather than record them, really strikes home.

B.C.   **BY JOHNNY HART**

By permission of Johnny Hart and Creators Syndicate, Inc.

Some years ago, Dupont offered a midwestern manufacturer the right to test a new synthetic rubber in automobiles. To compete with existing products, Dupont gave the manufacturer a 10 percent product discount. Chrysler agreed to try the new synthetic rubber in its shift seals, and after two years it decided to adopt the product for the entire line of vehicles. The manufacturer, looking to sell the synthetic rubber to all major automobile manufacturers, discovered that Dupont had perceived the discount as applying only to the test market (Chrysler) but not to the expanded market.

In early 1990, Mikhail S. Gorbachev met privately with U.S. Secretary of State James A. Baker III over the issue of German reunification. In return for Gorbachev's support, Baker assured the Russian leader that there would be no expansion of NATO's current jurisdiction eastward. However, nine years later the United States successfully pushed for expansion of NATO to include Poland, Hungary, and the Czech Republic—despite bitter protests from Russian officials that the expansion contradicted Baker's assurances, carefully worded as they might have been.

Guidelines for Getting It in Writing

Your own negotiations may not be as crucial as arms control or expansion of NATO, but you would nonetheless like as few surprises and disappointments as possible. Here are some guidelines for developing written agreements.

First, if it comes down to a choice between you or the other party handling the actual writing of the agreement, you generally are better off taking on this role. This can occur in two ways. One is for you to *take notes* throughout the negotiation, which leads naturally to the role of recording the agreement. Taking notes during a negotiation is always a good idea, since it not only helps you keep track of the issues, proposals, and tentative agreements but also implicitly signals that you are in charge of this negotiation. In a protracted negotiation, you can establish this role by sending memoranda of understanding summarizing progress to date.

A second way to undertake this function is by offering at the conclusion of the negotiation to *write up the agreement*. Most counterparts see this as a friendly gesture, one less task for them to do (and a menial, administrative task, at that). By taking responsibility for writing up the agreement, however, you gain more control over what goes into it (language, provisions, etc.). Once something appears in writing, it becomes more difficult for the other party to object and request changes.

This becomes clear the first time you negotiate an agreement with an organization that has a standard contract or boilerplate. A boilerplate contract is a preprinted agreement that can serve as the framework for a broad range of business deals. Many organizations use them, including mortgage companies, publishing firms, talent agencies, and construction companies. Additions and minor modifications are made per the terms of the particular negotiation under consideration. Generally, these changes or amendments must be initialed by both parties, to signify that both recognize and accept the changes.

A boilerplate can be intimidating because it is preprinted, a form of the authority-limit tactic that psychologically restricts modifications (particularly if the heading or other lettering is embossed on high-quality paper). In addition, a boilerplate undoubtedly contains all the terms, clauses, and conditions this organization wants in the contract (liabilities, penalties, etc.), and it is probably written in legalese, which is difficult for the layperson to interpret. You feel embarrassed to ask questions and, at the same time, afraid that if you don't ask you could be surprised later.

Unless it is your boilerplate or preprinted contract, avoid

being trapped by the other party's language and demands. A boilerplate connotes power or leverage, but one surprising way to reclaim that power is to mark it up. Make all the changes you feel are necessary. The markings and initials put your imprint on the agreement. Remember, everything is negotiable, even boilerplates.

If you are drawing up the agreement from scratch, it is not a bad idea to record the other party's gains or benefits first. This suggests concern for the other party and his interests. It also makes it more difficult for him to challenge any add-ons or riders that might follow (remember our one-for-the-road tactic?) for fear that he might lose the gains already recorded.

In starting from scratch, it is also important to capture not only the essence of the agreement in writing but the details as well. Too often, contracts or agreements lack specific information about roles, quantities, delivery dates, penalties, etc., which later creates confusion, animosity, or both. Basically, the document must answer who, what, when, where, and why. The language needs to be understandable, using specific quantities, times, dates, subcontractors, etc., and the provisions should be noncontradictory. Any references to other documents need to be checked out to make sure they do not contain surprising or contradictory claims.

Consider the following excerpt from an agreement written for the Valero Wine–Continental Glass negotiation presented in Chapter 6: "Valero Wine Company agrees to purchase 100,000 100-ml bottles from Continental Glass, to be delivered within ten days of this agreement. The purchase price is $15,000." How would you evaluate this agreement? What are three concerns that you have?

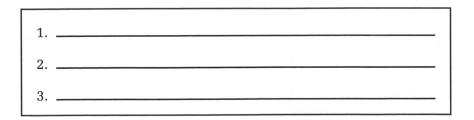

1. _____

2. _____

3. _____

There are quite a few areas of uncertainty:

* The agreement is specific about the amount, but it is unclear if this includes sales tax or shipping and handling charges, and who will pay the latter?
* Are the ten days allowed for delivery calendar days or working days?
* If Monday to Friday, are holidays excluded?
* What if the bottles are not delivered on time? Will a penalty be exacted?
* When is the payment due: at the time of delivery or within thirty days of invoicing?
* What happens if some bottles arrive damaged?
* Are there color, shape, and material expectations regarding the bottles?

Some contracts also include specifics regarding the conditions under which the agreement can be modified and the procedure to follow such as mediation or arbitration if a dispute arises that cannot be settled directly by the parties.

A poorly worded agreement can have a number of undesirable consequences, including misunderstandings resulting in inaction, unsatisfactory workmanship, reputation aspersion, and lawsuits. A number of sites on the World Wide Web offer boilerplates for a variety of contracts, including rental agreements, bills of sale, and contractor agreements, which provide examples of the information that might be included. If you are interested in seeing some samples, check out the Websites listed in the Resources section at the end of this book. Keep in mind, however, that there are many variations of these boilerplates, although they may contain much of the same information.

A third guideline is that the more important the negotiation (and the agreement that summarizes it), the more valuable it is to have someone look over the agreement before it is signed. What the author of an agreement understands implicitly may not be readily apparent to the other negotiating party—or to a judge or arbitrator who may have to decide someday whether the contract has been breached. A third party can sometimes spot vague references, omissions, or contradictions. If the negotiation involves a substantial commitment of time, resources, or money, it is always wise to employ a lawyer with expertise in this industry to write or review the terms. This is another form of authority limit, and most parties would expect their counterpart to request such a review in an important negotiation. A third party can ask questions and challenge the terms of an agreement on your behalf, allowing you to remain the good guy.

In fact, where a substantial investment is involved, you probably want to involve a lawyer or other third party throughout the process. Choose someone who is familiar not only with the business involved but also with the specific companies or organizations in the geographic area. Such an individual is more likely to have information regarding, say, the reputation of your prospective mortgage lender if you are buying property and know that this lender has a pattern of challenging appraisals or demanding a six-month escrow at closing time.

If the other party requests to have her business partner, accountant, or lawyer review the contract, limit how long this process takes. Put a deadline on when the review and signing is to be completed. (Remember the deadline tactic?) If there is any indication that this could be a recurring process, consider asking the lawyer(s) to join you in a final review and signing. This adds a ceremonial touch to an otherwise legal process.

Other Considerations

Even with all these precautions, you can find yourself on the short end if a contractor fails to complete his work or a supplier declares bankruptcy. As an added measure of protection, you might consider looking for a contractor or provider who is bonded. A bond is assurance of payment or fulfillment by a third party if the provider fails to meet contract obligations to the customer or client. There are many types of bonds, and your lawyer can help you understand which type of warranty or bond is most meaningful to you.

Some of the consequences of failing to adhere to one or more of these guidelines are shown in Table 13-1. These represent im-

Table 13-1: Common Problems With Agreements (and Their Consequences)

Problem	Potential Consequences
Not in writing	Misunderstandings or confusion Not perceived as binding Unenforceable
Prepared by other party	Unfamiliar terminology and clauses Tailored to other party's agenda
Lacks detail or specificity	Misunderstandings or confusion
Not reviewed by third party	Inconsistent with other documents and agreements Illegal or unenforceable

mediate consequences, which in turn can produce inefficiencies, missed opportunities, lawsuits, and reputation damage.

Although a written agreement provides significant protection in the United States and most other industrialized nations in the case of a breach of contract, in many less-developed countries a contract holds limited value. It is the friendship and honor between the two negotiators rather than a piece of paper that binds an agreement. In fact, in some cultures pushing a written agreement—particularly early in the negotiation—can do more harm than good. This is but one of the many differences that can be found in cross-cultural negotiations, the subject of the next chapter.

14

Cross-Cultural Negotiations

Time is money.

—Anonymous

Time is love.

—Graffiti outside the Louvre, Paris

In another, younger life, I fancied myself a designer of cooperative playground equipment. The idea was to design and build playground equipment not for individual play or parallel play, but so as to encourage cooperative play. That is, the equipment became more enjoyable as more children joined in its use, thus encouraging cooperation. I had convinced a small group of associates of the merits of a cooperative playground, and we set about to design the pieces.*

As luck would have it (and it was pure luck), I stumbled upon a Fulbright fellowship to Brazil to teach dispute resolution. Before departing, I learned of a man prominent in the International Play Association who lived in Rio de Janeiro. While in Rio, I decided to look him up to discuss the concept of a cooperative playground. It turned out that Ubiratan Correa was the director

---

*As an example, we designed a swing that basically joined two swings together, taking out one of the middle chains. So there were three chains supporting two seats, with the middle chain supporting both seats. It worked best when two people were facing in opposite directions, so that they were getting power in both directions. (I'm pumping when you are not, and you are pumping when I am not.) We called them "buddy swings."

of SESC, an organization charged with providing social opportunities for children and adults largely through multipurpose community centers.

Successful in locating Correa, I arranged a meeting at his office. We were joined by a child psychologist with a distinguished career of service in Brazil, Ethel Bauzer Medeiros. It was a friendly meeting, but I could see that they were at least initially skeptical and asked questions designed to test me as well as the concept. We drank *cafezinhos* (little coffees). Finally, I was invited to return for a visit to one of the centers that had recently been completed. I toured the site, met other people, and returned to Correa's office to learn about other centers and projects, including a $7 million leisure-recreation center designed for Nova Iguaçu, just outside Rio.

This meeting concluded with an invitation to return yet another day to visit Nova Iguaçu, where construction had begun, and to have lunch. Afternoon lunch is the major meal in Brazil, and Correa, two associates, and I went to a restaurant where the staff knew well both Correa and his tastes. We drank and we ate. We ate some more. There was absolutely no talk of business during the trip to Nova Iguaçu or during lunch. Then, just as we were finishing our *cafezinhos*, Correa said that the leisure-recreation center in Nova Iguaçu would need a playground. He wanted my group to design it. I should call for an appointment to stop by and pick up the blueprints.

I was delighted.

I was terrified.

But mostly, I was completely taken by surprise.*

Negotiation is challenging enough when you face someone you know and trust, someone who at least figuratively if not literally speaks your language. But when you move outside your cultural frame of reference, things can get very confusing and frustrating. Yet more than ever, the neighborhoods, communities,

---

*The playground was eventually built, although some designs were modified or adapted by the construction engineers. The buddy swings, for example, were built with small wooden seats rather than the leather-strap seats of our original design. These changes reflected cultural differences, limitations in our negotiated "written agreement" (the design specifications), and the complexities of a three-way, long-distance negotiation.

institutions, and organizations of the world are becoming multicultural. To be able to live and do business in the new global marketplace, one needs to be able to negotiate effectively across cultures.

Even though there are many similarities in terms of negotiation styles and customs around the world, there are also some fundamental differences. It is easy to be misled if you do not know the customs. In Brazil, for example, it is typical for your negotiating counterpart to give an immediate response of *no*. It almost doesn't matter what you are requesting—the answer is still *no*.* In Japan, on the other hand, the answer to any question is almost always *yes*. It is communicated with a nod, a bow, a smile, silence, or a flat-out "Yes."

You may be initially frustrated by the Brazilian no and relieved by the Japanese *yes*, but in fact there is a good chance that they mean exactly the opposite of what you think they mean. The Brazilian *no* is a way of testing and building relationship. It is a way of determining how important this negotiation is to you. The Japanese *yes* is a way of saving face for both parties; to tell someone *no* is to show disrespect. Therefore, in Brazil, *no, no, no, no, no, no, no* is likely to mean yes (if you push hard enough), while in Japan, *yes, yes, yes, yes, yes, yes* may very well mean *no* (or maybe, or I cannot say, or I do not understand, or I must go).

Many times we encounter difficulties in cross-cultural negotiations because we project our own behaviors, beliefs, and values onto others. That is, we interpret the behaviors of others through our own behavior in similar situations. Thus, if you mean *no* when you say *no*—particularly when you say no twice—you assume that others mean it as well. The people you encounter socially and professionally are interpreting your behaviors in the same way, through their experiences and expectations.

Here is an amusing illustration of this phenomenon. A

*In a charming experiment involving Japanese, American, and Brazilian negotiators, John Graham reported the average number of times various tactics were employed in thirty-minute bargaining sessions. The average number of *no*s per person used by Japanese negotiators over this time period was just under six, and the average number of *no*s used by American negotiators was nine, but the average number of *no*s for Brazilian negotiators was eighty-three!

young woman college student, newly arrived from India, described an encounter she had with a North American classmate
as they met while walking to and from campus, respectively. The
North American said "Hi. How are you?" as they were about to
pass on the street. The Indian woman stopped, assuming her
classmate was making a serious inquiry and wanted to learn
about her well-being. When the North American kept going, she
was stunned and confused. They were both, of course, operating
out of their respective cultural experiences.

Although it is difficult if not risky to generalize about cultures, it is perhaps more hazardous to proceed in ignorance with
negotiations involving parties from distant lands (or even distant
neighborhoods). With this in mind, let's discuss some aspects of
culture that often come into play during negotiations and that
might provide a framework for planning and executing future
cross-cultural encounters.

The Importance of Relationships

If you have been reading this book from beginning to end, as I
hope you have, it is easy to see how relationships play a central
role in the process of negotiation. The definitions presented in
the first chapter all implicitly (if not explicitly) suggest a second
party is needed for a negotiation to occur. The negotiation styles
presented in Chapter 7 are based on two dimensions, one of
which is concern for the other party or the relationship. The several examples you have read so far in this chapter all involve
relational behavior. Even though the importance placed on relationships in negotiations can vary from one individual to another
and one situation to another, there are often national or regional
similarities regarding relationships. This includes how much
time is devoted to developing a personal or business relationship
as well as how relationships are used throughout the negotiating
process.

As a general rule of thumb, negotiators from North America,
northwestern and Central Europe (for example, Great Britain,
Germany, Switzerland, Denmark, Sweden, the Netherlands), and
Australia and New Zealand focus more on task completion than

relational development. Consequently, their conversations are likely to move quickly into the nuts and bolts of a business negotiation (issues, terms). Throughout much of the rest of the world, including Latin America, Mediterranean Europe (Spain, Portugal, France, Italy, Greece), Africa, and Asia, relationships are central to the negotiating process. Far more time is spent getting to know the other party, his family, and his company through lunches, dinners, parties, site visits, etc. Negotiations are seen as more than agreements between individuals; negotiations join social systems (Table 14-1).

In these relation-based cultures, negotiations truly begin before any face-to-face encounter because one's social standing and organizational affiliation are very important. Furthermore, relationships represent an important source of power in Europe, Latin America, the Middle East, Africa, and Asia, and social systems are more hierarchical in these regions. It is who you know (social power) rather than what you know (expert power) that is important. The more people you know in prominent positions, the more sources of information and influence you have.

As a result, existing social and business contacts are often used as a means of gaining entry and initiating face-to-face negotiations in these cultures. Cold calling, which is commonplace in the United States, is infrequently employed. Instead, entry can be gained in one or more of these ways:

- Your surname is well known.
- You are directly or indirectly related.
- You have shared similar experiences (perhaps worked for the same company).
- You are attending the same function.
- You have a friend or acquaintance in common.
- A friend or colleague of the other party introduces you at a function.
- A friend or colleague of the other party calls or writes on your behalf.
- The other party knows someone who recommended that you call.

Looking back on my cooperative playground negotiation, I was lucky to get an appointment. I came with no referral. There

Table 14-1: Negotiating Styles Across Cultures

Characteristic	Region			
	North America, Northwestern and Central Europe, Australia, New Zealand	Mediterranean Europe, Latin America	Eastern Europe, Middle East, Africa	Pacific Rim
Relationships	Task-oriented Individualist Nonhierarchical social system Open entry Short-term focus	Relation-oriented Collectivist Hierarchical social system Network entry Medium-term focus	Relation-oriented Collectivist Hierarchical social system Network entry Long-term focus	Relation-oriented Collectivist Hierarchical social system Network entry Long-term focus
Behaviors and tactics	Informal or formal Social Monochronic time orientation Moderate initial demands and concessions Integrative (win-win) outcomes Direct discussions Logical, rational argumentation Sequential, linear processes Decentralized decision making Limited relational development	Formal, protocol Personal (touching, gifts) Polychronic time orientation Moderate initial demands and limited concessions Distributive (win-lose) outcomes Indirect discussions Emotional argumentation, debate Nonlinear processes Centralized decision making Moderate to extended development	Formal, protocol Personal (touching, gifts) Polychronic time orientation High initial demands and limited-to-high concessions Distributive (win-lose) outcomes Direct, indirect discussions Emotional, idealistic argumentation Nonlinear processes Centralized decision making Extended relational development	Formal, protocol Personal (reserved) Polychronic time orientation Limited initial demands and concessions Integrative (win-win) outcomes Indirect discussions No argumentation Linear processes Collective decision making Extended relational development
Agreements	Written agreements Detailed, specific Formal, legal	Oral or written agreements Broad, implied Informal and symbolic, or formal and legal	Oral or written agreements Broad, implied Informal, symbolic	Written agreements Broad, implied Formal, legal, and symbolic

was no one I knew who could introduce me; there wasn't even anyone we knew in common. For the most part, we connected through an organization, the International Play Association, and began to build a relationship over a series of meetings. As this experience suggests, it is possible to negotiate in relation-based cultures without referral or historical context. More time is needed up front, though, to establish rapport and trust. An initial call or meeting may be required to set up a formal meeting (a pattern that continued, in this case, with my subsequent visits to Brazil).

Finally, in those cultures where relationship is central to the negotiating process, the time horizon is markedly longer. That is, negotiators in Latin America, the Middle East, Africa, and Asia view negotiations as continuous rather than episodic. This time frame is reflected not only in how long negotiations take, but in the social contact that continues beyond the terms of the agreement. Correa, for example, continued to send me announcements of openings and events long after the cooperative playground project was completed.

Behaviors and Tactics

Although the negotiating style of North Americans is often informal, open, and direct, negotiators from northwestern Europe (Great Britain, for instance) may be less straightforward and direct. On the other hand, people from Latin America, Mediterranean Europe, Eastern Europe, the Middle East, and Africa can be both formal and personal. Formal introductions, titles, and business cards are frequently exchanged in the early stages of negotiating in these regions. However, subsequent meetings are likely to include hugging, kissing (on one or both cheeks), and gift giving as a sense of relationship develops.

The touching and proximity of these cultures can be most disarming to North Americans, northwestern Europeans, and Pacific Rim cultures. In the United States, for example, individuals typically maintain different spatial zones according to the type of communication. The *intimate zone* is the most proximate (approximately 0–18 inches) and is used for private conversations and comforting between relatives and close friends. The *personal zone* (approximately 18 inches to 4 feet) is used for general conversations with friends. The *social zone* extends this space still farther (approximately 4–12 feet) and is employed in conversations between strangers. And the *public zone* (beyond 12 feet) is used in lobbies, reception areas, and formal presentations. In Mediterranean Europe and Latin America, these zones are much closer, and there is a much higher incidence of touching during conversation.

When cultural opposites meet, it can be almost comical to watch. I recall observing one such encounter between two males. As the individual who preferred closer proximity while conversing closed the gap between the two, the individual who preferred larger zones would casually back away. The former was literally maneuvering the latter around the room, like partners locked in a new style of dance. Imagine a negotiation between a woman from Latin America and a man from North America. The woman's personal zone, with close proximity and touching to accentuate conversation, feels to the man like an intimate zone. Without a cultural road map, he might easily think that she is coming on to him.

The use of time also varies considerably across cultures. There are two common orientations to time: monochronic and polychronic. Cultures on monochronic time generally view time as a commodity. They save time, find time, spend time, lose time, waste time, and manage time. Time is money. People in monochronic cultures prefer to focus on one task at a time (linear orientation) and try to complete the task within a specified time period. Once the time period has expired, then they are likely to move on to the next task, whether or not the current task has been completed. Thus, keeping schedules, and keeping to timetables and schedules, is important in monochronic cultures. Most of the cultures of North America, northwestern and Central Europe, and Australia and New Zealand observe monochronic time.

In polychronic cultures, by contrast, time is viewed as relational. Rather than thinking about minutes being saved, spent, or wasted, the individual on polychronic time is engrossed in the moment. The meeting, encounter, or negotiation continues until the discussion, meal, or business is finished; polychronics are not bound by a schedule. Furthermore, people on polychronic time are able to engage in multiple activities "simultaneously." That is, they are easily interrupted or distracted, switching freely from one task to another. Latin America, Eastern and Mediterranean Europe, the Middle East, and Africa operate under polychronic time. Some Pacific Rim countries, such as Japan, operate on polychronic time in the development of relationships, yet are punctual in every other respect.

It is not hard to imagine how in a negotiation representatives from each culture would interpret and react to encountering the other's contrasting orientation to time. An individual from a monochronic culture who schedules a meeting for 2:00 to 3:00 P.M. with someone from a polychronic culture, promptly ends the meeting at 3:00 P.M. to attend to the next appointment even though their business has not concluded. The individual from the polychronic culture may think this is rude, or wonder how important the negotiation is to the other party.

If the roles are reversed and an individual from a polychronic culture calls the meeting, it is likely to start late but continue beyond the time allotted (if an end time is even specified).* The individual from the monochronic culture may feel upset that the meeting starts thirty to sixty minutes late, encouraged that the meeting extends beyond its scheduled time frame (though worried about getting to his or her next appointment), and annoyed by all the interruptions (phone calls taken, others entering the room with questions). The individual from the monochronic culture is probably confused and certainly wonders just how important this negotiation is to the other party.

In terms of specific behaviors and tactics, some cultures enjoy the give-and-take of bargaining and negotiation more than others do. Most Middle Eastern cultures, for example, make high initial demands with the expectation that there be a series of concessions. Individuals from many Eastern European cultures also

---

*A word of advice about your own timeliness when dealing with someone from a polychronic culture. Generally speaking, be punctual with polychronics, particularly in first encounters at their office (that is, where your need for them appears to exceed their need for you). Your punctuality is viewed by the other party as an early indicator of respect and the importance of the relationship.

tend toward high initial demands but are more limited in the concessions that they make. In these cultures negotiations are typically seen as distributive, with a winner and a loser. In keeping with their polychronic time orientation, argumentation may seem fragmented, circuitous, and nonlinear. Emotional appeals also are common, which is consistent with the importance of public image and relationships in these cultures. Compromise is seen as a sign of weakness, and one or two walkouts might be staged for effect.

In Mediterranean Europe and Latin America, initial demands and concessions may be more moderate, although the process is still seen as distributive (win-lose). Concessions often are made in private, to preserve one's honor. Argumentation is likely to be nonlinear and emotional, with overlapping conversations. These cultures place a high value on verbal skills in negotiating. As with Middle Eastern and Eastern European cultures, decision making is centralized in Mediterranean Europe and Latin America. Therefore, one must seek the individual with the authority to close the deal, or be prepared to go through the process again with someone else.

In contrast, many Pacific Rim negotiators seek integrative (win-win) outcomes. Their approach is to limit both demands and concessions. They employ tradition and indirect discussions as a way of maintaining the honor and face of *all* parties. Harmony and order is the key. Youth defers to age and wisdom. Sellers defer to buyers. That is, sellers trust buyers to look out for the interests of both parties. Decisions, however, are made collectively or consensually.

The goal also is an integrative outcome in North America, northwestern and Central Europe, and Australia and New Zealand. However, this is approached through direct discussions involving moderate initial demands and concessions. Logical, rational argumentation is employed to build one's case. The negotiating process is best described as sequential or linear. Unlike people from other cultures, individuals from these regions generally are given broad authority to negotiate agreements (decentralized decision making).

Once again, it is easy to imagine the confusion that might ensue in a negotiation involving uninitiated parties from different cultures, such as Japan and the United States. The Japanese representative seeks to learn everything possible about the company of the U.S. representative, whereas the latter seeks to jump into the issues and terms of the negotiation. If the Japanese representative is the seller, he assumes that the buyer is looking out for him. The U.S. representative presumes that each negotiator must look out for his own interests (especially the buyer, as the North American credo "Buyer beware!" so clearly warns), and the U.S. buyer perceives making demands and receiving concessions as simply outnegotiating his Japanese counterpart. The decentralized decision-making process common in the United States means that the representative is likely to have the authority to forge an agreement, but the collective or consensual decision-making process (called *ringi*) in Japan requires any number of individuals to sign off on the agreement. The Japanese silence or spoken or gestured "yes" is mistakenly interpreted to signify that we have a deal. The U.S. representative sees the negotiation as episodic (the relationship ends as soon as the terms of the agreement are completed), whereas the Japanese representative views the negotiation from an ongoing or long-term relational perspective.

Agreements

As suggested in the preceding chapter, the importance of written agreements varies considerably from country to country. To some extent, this is determined by the degree of relational orientation of the culture. The more time that is spent investigating and developing the relationship, the less importance is placed on formal contracts. Contracting also is a function of the legal system of a country, which can protect one's rights in lieu of relational commitment.

In North America, northwestern and Central Europe, and Australia and New Zealand, the legal systems are strong. Consequently, business negotiations are generally concluded with a written agreement or contract. The contract is probably specific and detailed so that a court of law can determine whether the terms have been violated. To some extent, this is true in Mediterranean Europe as well.

In Latin America, Eastern Europe, the Middle East, and Africa, one's social status and reputation are very important. Failure to meet an obligation is likely to travel very quickly through informal communication channels, making others wary of future dealings with this individual. A written agreement, therefore, is more symbolic of the relational bond that has been developed than it is a mechanism for enforcing rights. Consequently, written agreements are often couched in broad, general terms in these regions, since any future misunderstandings or disagreements will be worked out in the best interests of preserving the relationship.

Japan combines the best of both systems. Written agreements are seen as symbolic as well as legal, since relationships are central to the negotiating process and the legal system is very strong in Japan.

Other Cultural Differences

That's a quick overview of negotiation styles across cultures. There are differences beyond these factors, of course, and a host of subtleties. There are certain gestures, for example, that are considered endearing in one culture but offensive in another culture. The role of women as negotiators varies from culture to culture. Style of dress for business meetings is more formal in some cultures; it certainly varies in terms of ties and coats and hats. In some Latin American countries you kiss on one cheek; in other countries you kiss on both cheeks. In Japan, there are clearly defined kinds of bowing with different meanings. You might check the Resources section at the end of this book for more detailed information about specific countries and cultures.

In addition, there are subcultures within almost every culture that deviate from the broad generalizations described above. Negotiating in Washington, D.C., is different from doing so in New York City, which is also not the same in Los Angeles or Seattle or New Orleans. Within a major metropolitan area like Los Angeles, there are sure to be differences among Anglo American, African American, and Hispanic American populations. Many African Americans and Hispanic Americans, for example, are more relationship-oriented and polychronic with respect to meetings. The two largest ethnic groups in Malaysia—the Malays and the Chinese—have very different negotiating styles; Chinese Malaysians are generally more fast-paced, direct, and demanding than the Malays. In Sao Paulo, the business engine of Brazil, business attire is more formal and people are more punctual than in the city of Rio de Janeiro.

Although you cannot be expected to know the nuances of all cultures and subcultures from around the world, you are wise to appreciate the range of differences that exist. There is much to be said for traveling to other lands and spending time in other cultures. What is your experience in other cultures around the world?

* How many of the regions shown in Table 14-1 have you visited, and how much time have you spent in each region?
* In how many of these regions have you conducted business on behalf of a company or an organization?
* In how many of these regions have you made a social faux pas that you can recall?
* How many individuals have you dated from each of these regions, including parts of your native country?
* How many languages do you speak?

Lacking cultural or linguistic fluency (or even if you are fluent), you might consider forming a cross-cultural team for an important negotiation. Many organizations engaged in international business employ negotiating teams that include someone from their counterpart's culture. Using a negotiating team has numeric advantages (recall the confederates tactic), and having someone on the team from your counterpart's culture adds an element of legitimacy, signals to your counterparts that they will be understood, and helps you in interpreting and managing the process.

In cross-cultural negotiations, it is natural to assume that others think and act the same as you do. If they do not, it is almost as natural to ask "Why not?" and expect them to conform to your norms and customs. The general rule is "When in Rome, do as the Romans do" (although sometimes negotiators defer to the individual from the dominant culture). There are some behaviors, however, that are easier to accept and adopt than others, as we see in the next chapter.

15

Negotiation and Ethics

The truth is rarely pure, and never simple.
—Oscar Wilde

By this point, you have undoubtedly reacted (cognitively if not viscerally) to the range of tactics offered. Some tactics are more comfortable for you than others, and there may even be a few tactics that, under almost any circumstance imaginable, you would eschew. This brings us to the issue of ethics and ethical behavior.

Much has been written in the past few years about business ethics. The freewheeling 1980s and early 1990s produced a spate of well-publicized legal and ethical cases (Ivan Boesky; Charles Keating, Jr.; and Michael Milken in the United States come to mind; Eddy Tansil in Indonesia; and Yasuo Hamanaka in Japan, not to mention the Salt Lake City scandal involving the 2002 Winter Olympics bid), leading to public outcry for greater scrutiny of business practices, tougher sanctions for those who break the law, and training and education for current and future business leaders. There are now quite a few books and journals on business responsibility, moral conduct, and ethical behavior, and a growing number of centers and institutes to study these subjects.

When it comes to negotiation, information is everything. Consequently, some people operate fast and loose with facts, figures, promises, and proposals. They tell you what you *want* to hear, but not necessarily what you deserve to hear. Others simply don't give you all the information you need to make a wise decision. Still others cannot help but tell the truth, the whole truth, and nothing but the truth. In fact, they are so aboveboard in their negotiations that they cannot bring themselves even to tell "little white lies" (designed to protect the innocent).

It is not my intent to convince you to recalibrate your moral compass, or to suggest that there might be something in the laws of nature that recommends a universal code of ethics. What is important is that you understand your ethical limits—what behavior you find acceptable and what you deem not acceptable—and that you recognize the boundaries of others. This helps you realize the types of situation that might be difficult for you, that perhaps you should even avoid, because of the greater latitude your opponent allows himself.

You probably have a sense of your ethical convictions. The negotiation exercises in this book have given you additional insight into your beliefs and practices. To take this a bit further, complete the short questionnaire below on your perceptions of various negotiation behaviors. Answer the questions honestly, thinking in general terms about your negotiating experiences, beliefs, and behavior.

Incidents in Negotiation

Here are a number of negotiating tactics. These tactics primarily address how honest you are in negotiation. There are no "right answers" as to what is the right or wrong thing to do, so please be candid in your answers.

You are about to enter into a negotiation. You are negotiating for something that is important to you. Please think about each tactic below, and then rate each one on the two scales that follow by putting an X on each scale.

1. Promise that good things will happen to your opponent if he or she gives you what you want, even if you know that you can't (or won't) deliver those good things once the other's cooperation is obtained.

a. How appropriate is the tactic to use in a negotiation?

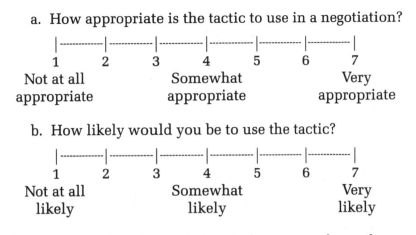

b. How likely would you be to use the tactic?

| ------------ | ------------ | ------------ | ------------ | ------------ | ------------ |
1   2   3   4   5   6   7
Not at all   Somewhat   Very
likely   likely   likely

2. Make an opening demand that is far greater than what one really hopes to settle for.

a. How appropriate is the tactic to use in a negotiation?

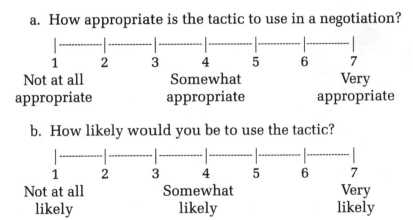

b. How likely would you be to use the tactic?

| ------------ | ------------ | ------------ | ------------ | ------------ | ------------ |
1   2   3   4   5   6   7
Not at all   Somewhat   Very
likely   likely   likely

3. Gain information about an opponent's negotiating position by cultivating his or her friendship through expensive gifts, entertaining, or personal favors.

a. How appropriate is the tactic to use in a negotiation?

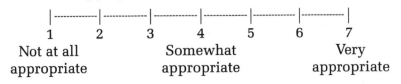

b. How likely would you be to use the tactic?

```
|------------|------------|------------|------------|------------|------------|
1            2            3            4            5            6            7
```
Not at all   Somewhat   Very
likely   likely   likely

4. Talk directly to the people your opponent reports to, or is accountable to, and try to encourage them to defect to your side.

a. How appropriate is the tactic to use in a negotiation?

```
|------------|------------|------------|------------|------------|------------|
1            2            3            4            5            6            7
```
Not at all   Somewhat   Very
appropriate   appropriate   appropriate

b. How likely would you be to use the tactic?

```
|------------|------------|------------|------------|------------|------------|
1            2            3            4            5            6            7
```
Not at all   Somewhat   Very
likely   likely   likely

5. Intentionally misrepresent factual information to your opponent to support your negotiating arguments or positions.

a. How appropriate is the tactic to use in a negotiation?

```
|------------|------------|------------|------------|------------|------------|
1            2            3            4            5            6            7
```
Not at all   Somewhat   Very
appropriate   appropriate   appropriate

b. How likely would you be to use the tactic?

```
|------------|------------|------------|------------|------------|------------|
1            2            3            4            5            6            7
```
Not at all   Somewhat   Very
likely   likely   likely

Evaluating Your Negotiation Preference Ratings

So, how do you interpret your ratings? One way is to rank the five behaviors from most appropriate to least appropriate. Which tactic do you consider most appropriate? Which do you consider least appropriate? Most individuals see some behaviors as more appropriate than others. That is, the behaviors are usually not all rated the same (all 1s or all 4s or all 7s). Furthermore, individuals generally find traditional competitive-bargaining behaviors, such as exaggerating an opening demand (the second behavior listed), the most appropriate behavior and the one they are most likely to use.

A second way of evaluating your ratings is by comparing them with the mean or average ratings of a sample from the larger population. One such sample, of several hundred college students attending MBA programs in the United States, produced the results shown on the next two pages. The mean values for men and women respondents are indicated on each scale by M and F, respectively. Transfer your Xs from the scales on the previous pages to the scales below to compare results more easily.

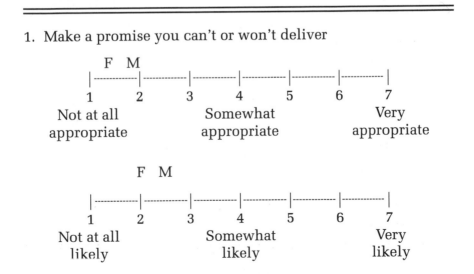

1. Make a promise you can't or won't deliver

```
        F  M
|-------|-------|-------|-------|-------|-------|
1       2       3       4       5       6       7
Not at all      Somewhat                Very
appropriate     appropriate             appropriate
```

```
        F  M
|-------|-------|-------|-------|-------|-------|
1       2       3       4       5       6       7
Not at all      Somewhat                Very
likely          likely                  likely
```

2. Exaggerate your opening demand

F M

```
|------------|------------|------------|------------|------------|------------|
1            2            3            4            5            6            7
```
Not at all   Somewhat   Very
appropriate   appropriate   appropriate

F   M

```
|------------|------------|------------|------------|------------|------------|
1            2            3            4            5            6            7
```
Not at all   Somewhat   Very
likely   likely   likely

3. Feign friendship for information

F   M

```
|------------|------------|------------|------------|------------|------------|
1            2            3            4            5            6            7
```
Not at all   Somewhat   Very
appropriate   appropriate   appropriate

F   M

```
|------------|------------|------------|------------|------------|------------|
1            2            3            4            5            6            7
```
Not at all   Somewhat   Very
likely   likely   likely

4. Encourage others to defect

F M

```
|------------|------------|------------|------------|------------|------------|
1            2            3            4            5            6            7
```
Not at all   Somewhat   Very
appropriate   appropriate   appropriate

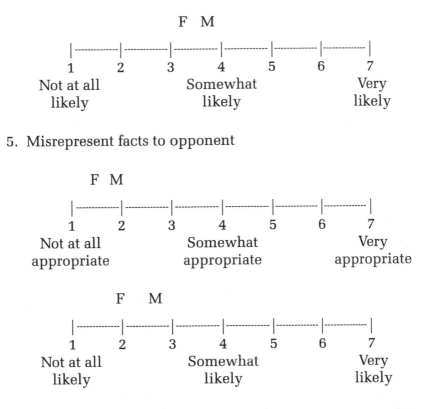

5. Misrepresent facts to opponent

Before you get too excited about these comparisons, let me point out that this sample of respondents selected the full range of values along these scales. That is, there were individuals from this sample who rated the appropriateness of misrepresenting facts to an opponent as not at all appropriate (1); others who rated this behavior 2; still others who rated it 3, 4, 5, 6; and some who selected 7 (very appropriate). The same range was found for the other four behaviors, and for the respondents' ratings of their likely use of these five behaviors. So there are no right or wrong responses, just different responses.

You probably noticed that the women from this sample held a higher standard than the men (that is, they felt the behaviors were less appropriate and they indicated that they would be less likely to use them). This is a typical finding in studies of ethics. You should also know that older individuals (in their forties and beyond) generally have a higher standard than younger people (twenties and thirties). Keep in mind that the sample consisted of graduate business students whose average age was about thirty, and mostly natives of the United States.

Where do your choices (Xs) fall on these scales? Are they consistently higher or lower than the means for your gender? How much higher or lower? If your rating is more than two points on either side of a mean value, it is outside the range of most respondents from this sample.

You might also notice that, for this sample of respondents, likely use was slightly higher than perceived appropriateness on each scale. This also is not an uncommon finding. Generally, people recognize that their behaviors are a bit more liberal than their attitudes. In fact, for many people ethics is a relative concept (that is, situation-specific). For example, if a particular negotiation is critical to your financial solvency, are you inclined to alter your negotiation behavior? What if you know that the other party is a very skillful negotiator? What if the other party has a reputation as an unethical negotiator? What if you will never see the other person again?

The flexibility or elasticity of one's ethics is determined by personal characteristics and cultural influences. In terms of personal characteristics, there are three broad categories of ethical reasoning: egocentric, relational, and principled (see Table 15-1). Those who fall into the egocentric category are concerned with

Table 15-1: Three Categories of Ethical Reasoning

Category	Perspective	Ethical Flexibility or Elasticity
Egocentric	Maximize personal gains, minimize personal losses	High
Relational	Conform to social norms and expectations	Moderate
Principled	Follow principles that transcend social convention	Low

personal gains and personal losses. They view ethics as an exchange, without regard for the psychological interests of others. What is right or appropriate is relative, since what matters is one's personal payoff.

Those individuals who fall into the relational category base their ethics on the norms and values of their peers. How do your actions affect others? What is expected of you by your family, friends, and colleagues? If your social circle says that a behavior is acceptable, then it is acceptable.

Finally, there are those individuals who base their ethics on a set of principles. These principles might include the laws of nature, respect for human dignity, or a universal code. Regardless of changes in the majority opinion of society, those who fall into the principled category hold to their fundamental principles. Therefore, they are the least likely to change their attitudes or behaviors, including under challenging or unfavorable negotiating conditions. Of course, this type of individual may also hold stubbornly to his or her position in a negotiation, standing on principle.

Culture also is an important determinant of ethical behavior, particularly for the vast majority of people whose reasoning is guided by social or relational expectations. The culture or shared beliefs of a people determine the social norms and laws that govern behavior. You may have discovered that certain behaviors or practices are more commonly accepted in some cultures than in others. Bribery, to take a vivid example, is standard practice in some countries; you simply cannot get anything accomplished unless you pay someone "under the table." If you are in another culture where such payments are commonplace, what do you do? What are your ethical standards, and how flexible or elastic are they?

These are critical questions, since encountering others with lower standards or more flexibility may put you at a negotiating disadvantage. A negotiating counterpart from such a culture may not even be aware that exaggerating an opening offer or making promises he cannot or will not keep or offering money for information is something that you would find unethical. By the same token, if your standards can best be characterized as "anything goes" or "the ends justify the means," you might encounter some individuals who abhor your beliefs and practices . . . and who refuse to do business with you.

A friend told me an anecdote that illustrates what can happen when cultures with different ethical norms meet. He and his family had recently moved to the United States from a developing country, one in which bribes are relatively commonplace. His wife, who was still learning English, was out alone one day running errands when she was involved in an automobile accident. The accident wasn't serious—no one appeared hurt—but there was some damage to the two cars involved. She was not at fault in the accident; nonetheless it was upsetting. A police car arrived at the scene, and her immediate concern was "Who do I pay?" That is, which officer or official does she pay to ensure that the accident gets recorded accurately? In her home country, the written account of an accident is central to any future claims, and involved parties often paid officials to ensure a favorable report.

If you expect to engage in business practices throughout the world, it might be to your advantage to know which countries have a reputation for high ethical standards and which countries do not. An organization called Transparency International puts out an index each year based on a variety of international surveys of businesspeople as to which are the most corrupt countries in the world. They define corruption as misuse of public power for private benefit, including bribery, acceptance of kickbacks, and embezzlement. A recent Transparency International index included perceptions of eighty-five countries.

Which countries do you think ranked in the bottom five on this list (that is, the five countries perceived to be the most corrupt)?

Most corrupt

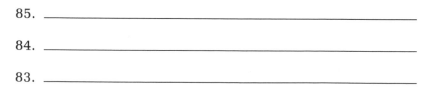

85. _____

84. _____

83. _____

82. _____

81. _____

How about the least corrupt?

Least corrupt

1. _____

2. _____

3. _____

4. _____

5. _____

The country perceived by those surveyed to be the most corrupt was Cameroon (eighty-five), followed by Paraguay, Honduras, Tanzania, and Nigeria (these last two tied for eighty-first/eighty-second). The country perceived to be the least corrupt was Denmark (number one on the list), followed by Finland, Sweden, New Zealand, and Iceland. You may be wondering where the United States ranked in this survey. It was tied for seventeenth/eighteenth.*

Dealing with corruption is a challenge for individuals who hold a higher standard. This challenge clearly illustrates one aspect of the Golden Rule of negotiation: an individual is not going to be willing to negotiate with you unless you are willing to help him or her. How might one handle this dilemma? You could, of course, adapt the old bromide to read "When in Cameroon, do as the Cameroonians do." You might also stand on principle and hope that your counterparts acquiesce to your value system. Another approach is to employ some form of authority limit, or sug-

*For information on Transparency International's survey on corruption in business transactions, check out their Website (www.transparency.de).

gest the legal consequences to you back home if bribes are paid. If there truly are higher authorities, gaining their permission may relieve you of both responsibility and angst. Learning more about your counterparts, including how steadfast they are in their requests for bribes as well as how you can hurt them, also helps.

16

Measuring Your Progress Again

The Logan Telecommunications–RJW Properties Negotiation

If you think you can, you can. And if you think you can't, you're right.
  —Mary Kay Ash, founder of Mary Kay Cosmetics

It's time to check your progress once more. This negotiation requires a bit more time—approximately thirty minutes—and I encourage you to pick a new negotiating partner/opponent, not one of the individuals with whom you have already negotiated within the context of this book. If you can find someone from another culture to negotiate with you, all the better.

This negotiation involves Logan Telecommunications and a commercial properties company called RJW Properties, Inc. You will represent Logan, a company that is looking to expand into a new regional market. You want to lease some commercial space on its behalf to establish a cellular telephone service in this new market.

As with the previous negotiations that you undertook in this book, each party to the negotiation has his or her confidential information. In this case, however, there are more than one or two issues to negotiate. In fact, there are seven explicit issues that are important to you. For each issue there is a specified range of outcomes. You receive a certain number of points, depending on the outcome that you are able to negotiate. Since some issues are more important to you than they are to the other party (and thus worth more points), you and your opponent have your own scoring tables.

Because this is a more complex negotiation in terms of the number of issues involved, the first of our three fundamental questions of negotiation ("What do I want?") is particularly important. Consider the seven issues and their point values carefully, prioritizing your "wants" before launching into face-to-face negotiations. Think about how you are going to go after your wants and how to learn about the other party's needs.

Enough hints. Find a negotiating partner. Read the confidential background information for Logan Telecommunications below, while your counterpart reads the confidential background information for RJW Properties found in Appendix C. After you have both completed your readings and are ready, introduce yourself as the Logan representative and begin the negotiation. Your counterpart at RJW Properties has a lease agreement form for recording the terms of your agreement (that is, what you agree to for each of the issues).

LOGAN TELECOMMUNICATIONS
(Confidential Facts)

Logan Telecommunications is a fifteen-year-old telecommunications company that has grown rapidly over the past three years. Logan provides several telecommunications services, one of which is cellular telephone service. It is in this area—as a cellular telephone provider—that Logan has grown most rapidly in recent years and the company sees its future.

There are several geographic regions Logan believes to have the greatest growth potential for the cellular market. As a Logan representative, you have been assigned the task of finding and leasing commercial space for these ventures. In general, there is some urgency in leasing commercial space, renovating it, and becoming operational, since one or two other service providers are competing for the same cellular customers in each region.

The first region in which Logan would like to expand has a number of commercial properties, but only a few prime locations. You have found what you believe to be the ideal location for your operation, a 3,000 square foot commercial space managed by a company called RJW Properties, Inc. You would like to lease this office space, plus some parking, for one or two years at a reasonable rate.

The lease price is an important issue for you, but there are, in fact, at least seven issues that have to be resolved to complete this negotiation:

1. Cost per square foot
2. Renovation of space
3. Utilities
4. Length of lease
5. Parking
6. Furnishings
7. Advanced payment

For each of these issues, there are several possible outcomes. For each outcome that you negotiate, you receive a specific number of points. These points reflect how important the Issue and outcome are to you and your company. These considerations are shown in the Scoring Key:

SCORING KEY FOR LOGAN TELECOMMUNICATIONS NEGOTIATION

Issue	Negotiated Outcome	Point Value
Cost per square foot	$50	900
	$60	750
	$70	600
	$80	450
	$90	300
Renovation of space	No rooms renovated	0
	One room	400
	Two rooms	500
	Three rooms	600

Issue	Negotiated Outcome	Point Value
Utilities included	None	200
	Water and sewer	300
	Water, sewer, and electricity	400
Length of lease	One year	500
	Two years	450
	Three years	300
	Four years	200
Parking available	No cars	100
	One car	300
	Two cars	500
	Three cars	600
	Four cars	650
Furnishings	None	100
	Refrigerator and stove	150
Advanced payment	One month's rent	800
	Six months' rent	600
	One year's rent	300

Your counterpart at RJW Properties has his or her own scoring key, which is different from yours. Do not share your scoring key with your counterpart, since this is confidential information. Once you have completed your negotiation, record and sign your agreement on the form provided to the RJW Properties representative. Your goal is to negotiate the highest score possible.

Evaluating the Negotiation

After you complete the negotiation, record your agreement, and sign the contract, it is all right to view the confidential information held by the RJW Properties representative. In doing so, notice that the maximum points possible for each representative is 4,000, while the minimum is 1,200 points.

The most important issue for you is the cost per square foot (900 points maximum), followed by the advance payment (800 points maximum). The renovation of space is also important, since the difference between having no rooms renovated and at least one room renovated is 400 points. For the representative from RJW Properties, the cost per square foot, the length of the lease, and advance payment each has the potential of yielding 900 points.

Typically, a representative of Logan Telecommunications negotiates somewhere between 2,900 and 3,300 points. But this case isn't so much about points as it is about how you approach the negotiation. The final numbers take care of themselves if you attend to the process of negotiation, one that doesn't end when you sign the contract.

This is a negotiation in which relationship building is very important. You are going to be landlord and tenant. There are things that come up (such as renovations, repairs, parking problems, subleasing) that will require special assistance and cooperation from RJW Properties. You do not want to get off on the wrong foot, hammering out an agreement that makes RJW Properties feel it owes you no future considerations. More than anything, you want to build a working relationship.

Many of the behaviors of highly skilled negotiators described in Chapter 5 are not only appropriate but imperative in this case, beginning with asking open-ended questions. By asking, for example, "What can you tell me about your property?" "How has business been lately?" "What sort of tenant are you looking for?" "What are the important issues for you in signing this lease?" you can learn a great deal about what is important and, by lack of mention, not so important to the RJW Properties representative.

Since multiple issues are involved, some of which are more important to the other party than to you, there are probably some sticking points where you want to resort to bargaining. Along the way, testing understanding and summarizing discussions is a valuable behavior to employ, while offering counterproposals, disagreeing before explaining your reasoning, defending your position, counterattacking, and using value statements (irritators) are behaviors that should be avoided or used with caution.

As a strategy, some negotiators like to build momentum by gaining agreement on the "easy" issues first. This creates an investment, which the other party may find difficult to walk away from once more difficult issues must be addressed. Other negotiators are not so quick to concede the easy issues, since they can be useful bargaining points later on (remember the strawman tactic?).

In any case, you probably found that the seven issues were more than you could keep straight in your head. Who kept notes during the negotiation: you, your counterpart, or both of you? If you know the other party has a boilerplate (agreement form), you may concede recording and control. There is no reason why you cannot take your own notes; did you? Many day-to-day negotiations involve only one or two issues each, but imagine what a labor-management or international trade negotiation (such as the North American Free Trade Agreement) is like, with all the stakeholders and scores of issues. Managing such complicated negotiations requires that external memory be employed (blackboards, flip charts) or that the set of issues be controlled by restricting initial attention to those most important to you and your opponent.

Keep in mind that with a complex negotiation involving experienced negotiators, you have to expect that you will gain some things and lose some things, particularly where the issues and positions are fairly well known. Such a negotiation is not judged by the number of issues won or lost, but by the value of the final agreement. Some negotiators are unable to complete this Logan–RJW Properties negotiation because one or both negotiators want their way with every issue. This negotiation, almost by design, calls for trade-offs (although they don't have to be made at the front end of the negotiation).

In the event that you were unable to come to an agreement, how did the negotiation end? Generally speaking, it is always a good idea to leave the door open for the other party to contact you if an agreement cannot be reached. This suggests that there are no hard feelings and that you are willing to continue to work toward an agreement. It preserves a sense of relationship. If the other party should contact you, it also suggests that the other party believes there is some way that you can help (or hurt) him or her.

Self-Assessment

Before we move on, let's do a self-assessment as we did with the Valero Wine–Continental Glass and Carson Enterprises negotiations in Chapters 6 and 11, respectively. Answer the following questions about yourself and your counterpart, and ask the representative from RJW Properties to do the same. In responding to the questions, think about everything that you have learned thus far about the negotiating process. After you record your perceptions, take a few minutes to give each other feedback.

What do you think you did well in this negotiation?

1. _____
2. _____
3. _____
4. _____

What do you think you should do differently in the next negotiation?

1. _____
2. _____
3. _____
4. _____

What do you think the other representative did well in this negotiation?

1. _____

2. _____

3. _____

4. _____

What do you think the other representative should do differently in his or her next negotiation?

1. _____

2. _____

3. _____

4. _____

You might find it interesting to go back and see what you recorded for the Valero Wine–Continental Glass and Carson Enterprises negotiations, as well as what your negotiating partners/opponents in those negotiations thought were your strengths and weaknesses. What strategies, tactics, and behaviors have you learned and applied as a representative of Logan Telecommunications that you did not employ in the earlier negotiations? What things did you do well in all three negotiations? What things do you still need to change?

17

Negotiating for the
*Un*natural Negotiator

Everything comes to him who hustles while he waits.
—Thomas A. Edison

Let's face it. Some people are much better at negotiating than the rest of us. It could be that they grew up in a culture where bargaining and negotiation were tightly woven into the fabric of life. It could be that they grew up in a family of five brothers and sisters, where every trip to the bathroom was a negotiation. Or it could be that they simply come by it naturally; it is part and parcel of their persona. Whatever the reasons, they have the gift, particularly in face-to-face encounters.

What about the rest of us? What if you are not a natural negotiator? What if you discover after reading this book that you still have difficulty in face-to-face negotiations, particularly if your counterpart is a very skilled negotiator? What can you do to create a situation that gives you a chance, if not an advantage, against the best negotiators?

Here are some suggestions that not only give you an advantage but enhance your confidence to make all the other tips and suggestions work even better.

Scout Your Opponent

The more you know about your counterpart—his or her business (age, history, competitors, current market), his or her problems, concerns, needs, triumphs, disappointments, dreams, friends, negotiating style—the better off you are. Getting this information is not as difficult as you might imagine. You can learn a lot about the market through newspaper articles, which can be searched manually or with the help of computer resources. The Internet and the World Wide Web are enormous sources of information on almost any topic imaginable.

If you are thinking of buying or leasing real estate, take a walk through the neighborhood that interests you. Visit a building or two in the neighborhood, and find out what the going prices are and how people like the area. You might even walk through the building that you want to lease or buy, observe who comes and goes, and chat with a few people.

Before I bought my first cooperative, I called the people who had rented it previously. I told them that I was interested in buying the unit and wanted to know how they liked it. I asked a lot of open-ended questions, as well as a few close-ended questions about things that concerned me. Because they had nothing to lose by being forthright, I was able to learn a great deal and have a few things confirmed. I raised some of these concerns with the owner (without revealing my source) very inquisitively, much like the playing-dumb tactic.

To learn something about a prospective counterpart's negotiating style and tactics, talk with someone who has negotiated with her recently, preferably on similar issues. Is the prospective counterpart collaborative, accommodating, or a toughie? What type of toughie? What tactics does she prefer? When the community affairs director of a resort town was called in one day and told she was going to be let go, she contacted a friend who had negotiated a release from his position just months earlier with the same city manager. She learned that the city manager would give a reasonable severance package but would demand a token concession in return. During the negotiation she quickly identified what token concession he would go to war over and she made that her strawman in a very successful negotiation.

In many cases, just knowing more about the object of your negotiation and the party with whom you are about to negotiate gives you added confidence. Any information gleaned from a face-to-face negotiation can validate what you already know, or provide insight into the veracity of your counterpart.

Develop a BATNA

Perhaps the greatest peace of mind for any negotiator comes with having a best alternative to a negotiated agreement. Confidence that one has a BATNA—a real, true alternative—cannot help but be communicated nonverbally to the other party. Your posture, distance, voice, and eyes all reflect your comfort in knowing that if this negotiation falls through, you have an alternative that is at least acceptable. (Which is not to say that you do not work toward an agreement, looking beyond positions to interests, trying to enhance your situation.)

Sometimes the status quo can serve as your BATNA if the need that you seek to satisfy isn't overwhelming. Generally you are better off with one solid alternative, however, rather than several alternatives, none of which really meets your needs. The more important the negotiation is to you, the more important it is for you psychologically and strategically to have a BATNA. In fact, there may be times when you will want to tell the other party your options, as a way of building trust or moving beyond an impasse. Some negotiating counterparts assume that you don't have an option if you don't mention it (and if you don't, then these same counterparts still might detect the fact in your nonverbals).

Also, be aware that BATNAs can change during the course of a negotiation. If a company makes an offer to hire you away from your present employer, for example, you might go back to your employer with this information. If you want to take the offer, you strengthen your BATNA by getting your current employer to offer an incentive to keep you. On the other hand, if you are willing to stay with your current employer, you can use the company making the offer as your BATNA.

Whether or not you feel comfortable playing one side against the other depends on your personality (style, risk propensity). But you will most assuredly feel more relaxed and confident if you have an alternative or fallback in any negotiation. So, if you don't have a natural alternative prior to engaging in your target negotiation, create one. Find a worthy competitor of your negotiating counterpart and strike up a parallel negotiation. In so doing, you increase your options as well as insight into your counterpart's needs.

Choose a Time and Location That Are Favorable to You

Like all other behavior, negotiation takes place within an environment that can help or hinder interaction and outcome. Being in a place that is unfamiliar can make you feel unsure of yourself and uncomfortable. When you go to an appliance store, you are negotiating on the salesperson's turf. Unless you are killing time or window shopping, you have already communicated to him or her, implicitly, that this negotiation is important enough for you to travel some distance. Depending on the day of the week, traffic, and weather conditions, the investment or sacrifice you have made to get there speaks volumes. If the store is busy, the salesperson clearly has other options and can quickly turn to them if the negotiation isn't going anywhere.

An office or conference room also can be intimidating. You wait outside someone's office or alone in the conference room until he is ready to see you. After all, he is an important and busy person. Once inside the other party's office, you are acutely aware that he is sitting comfortably behind a desk, perhaps in a plush leather chair, while you are less comfortably seated, positioned to see the diplomas and certificates adorning the wall. (Herb Cohn, the infamous chief of Columbia Pictures, was alleged to sit on a "throne"; to go into his office meant you were actually sitting at a lower level, looking up.) All the resources of the company are at your counterpart's disposal, including personnel. In addition, if you meet in someone else's office, telephone calls can interrupt the session, and "another meeting" can be offered as a convenient excuse to curtail discussions.*

*If you are a confident negotiator, going into an office that generally favors the other party can actually work to your advantage. Expecting you to be awestruck if not intimidated like most everyone else, you may actually score points by displaying calm, certitude, and wit under such conditions. Your opponent begins to wonder if perhaps there are some ways that you might be able to help him or her, given your self-confidence and style.

A location disadvantage need not be deliberate. Early in my career, I interviewed for an executive director's position at a Midwestern university. The university was establishing an institute on environmental dispute resolution, and the new director would be involved in mediation, training, program development, and fund-raising. I flew in for an interview, and there were four or five people in the conference room where the interview was to occur. I sat in an overstuffed chair that enveloped me. I could not easily move my arms to gesture. I shrank. When a disagreement arose among the interviewers over some of the responsibilities of the new position, I remained passive rather than becoming the facilitator or mediator they were undoubtedly seeking in an applicant.

If possible, choose a place to negotiate that puts you at ease. More than likely, such a place allows for comfortable seating, quiet conversation, and few distractions or interruptions. If you can't control the location (for example, you are going to contest a traffic ticket, so the meeting is in the judge's courtroom), you might at least want to visit the site prior to your negotiation to gain some familiarity with the surroundings and the procedures.

If at all possible, you should also pick a time that is best for you to negotiate. Going to a store on the day after Thanksgiving in the United States to do any type of negotiation is ludicrous. Going on other holidays and on weekends is also likely to ensure that clerks and salespeople have little time or incentive to bargain or negotiate—there are too many eager buyers for them to choose from. At many retail stores, there are certain times near the end of the month or year when employees can earn special commissions by making one or two more sales. If new cars are about to arrive for the coming year, auto salespeople have more incentive to sell off last year's models. Some days of the week and hours of the day are better than others to call an office for assistance, information, or a favor. (Avoid Mondays, for example, because these are organizing and meeting days for many people.) You may want to think twice about taking a telephone call that catches you by surprise, as you may not be at your best if you haven't thought through the issues or are otherwise distracted. Telephone negotiations have some other risks, which are discussed below.

The Medium Is the Message:
Choose Your Medium

There are many ways to communicate, each with its own advantages and disadvantages. These include letters, facsimiles, videos, telephone calls, voice-mail messages, e-mail messages, and face-to-face encounters. Each medium has a place in the negotiation process.

Communication scholars talk of media in terms of "information richness." Some media can convey more information than others. Generally speaking, face-to-face exchanges are highest in information richness, because nonverbal communication is part of every face-to-face encounter. Nonverbal communication includes proximity, posture, hand gestures, facial expressions, and vocal intonations. Salespeople, for example, are very comfortable with face-to-face negotiations, because they have learned how to send and interpret the nonverbal messages that can make them effective negotiators.

At the other extreme, short written messages tend to be low in information richness. All of the subtle nonverbal information is missing (remember, information is the key to negotiation). Unless you precede e-mail messages, for example, with face-to-face meetings that establish a sense of the relationship and a basis for interpretation, it is difficult to persuade or influence someone with this medium.

There is another factor to consider in choosing a medium: the advantage or disadvantage that it may give the other party. Telephone calls, for example, are relatively low in information richness; it is also easy for the party on the other end of the line to be "called away" or to just say no and hang up. In addition, there is often a direct relationship between the time and inconvenience involved in getting to a meeting and the amount of time devoted to it. If you have to travel one or two hours to get to a meeting, the other party probably will accord you proportionately more time than if the trip takes only ten minutes. Since telephone calls seldom require much effort from the caller, the other party may feel little obligation to stay on the line. (Telemarketers know all this and frequently try to get you to answer yes to a series of short questions—"You enjoy living in San Francisco? You like to take advantage of the city's cultural attractions? You support the arts?"—before quickly getting to the real question, which involves your credit card.)*

What works best, however, depends on what makes you most comfortable. If you are a good writer, send a résumé and samples of your work through the mail (keeping in mind that the length of the letter or other communiqué often prompts an equally short or lengthy reply). If you have trouble in heated, face-to-face encounters, limit that type of engagement. If your sense of humor might be taken the wrong way, reduce the risk by thinking ahead what you want to say, calling when the other party is likely to be away, and leaving a concise voice-mail message. You may not be able to avoid certain media altogether, but try to maximize your use of those that favor you and minimize your use of others.

Establish Limits (Authority, Financial)

When you go into an automobile dealership, slam some car doors, kick some tires, and finally find a car that catches your fancy, the salesperson invariably tells you that he has to check with the manager before the deal is closed. Much like using an agent, the manager (whom you may never see) is someone who can draw the line in a negotiation without relational consequences. You can't get mad at the salesperson because it was the manager who drew the line. This line can keep the salesperson from making too sweet an offer, or it can force the salesperson to test your desire for a car . . . this car!

Some people can set their own limits (for example, those

---

*One of the advantages of telephone negotiations, however, is that you can use notes without the other party's knowledge. Once an acquaintance has been made through one or more face-to-face encounters, media such as letters, e-mail, and telephone negotiations allow you the luxury of thinking through your ideas, organizing them, and jotting them down before engaging the other party. Unless a negotiation is viewed as complex or you are acting as an agent for others, using notes during a face-to-face negotiation may suggest lack of confidence, proficiency, or resourcefulness.

individuals whose temperament is based on risk avoidance and a strong concern for preserving self-interest). They can enter a negotiation having decided that they are only going to spend X dollars, or that they are only going to sign a contract if they can get A, B, and C. The age of credit card mania has clearly demonstrated, however, that many, many people buy first and do the arithmetic later (if at all). Setting a limit, or having another party set a limit, can provide the kind of boundary that keeps most of us from being swept away during a negotiation.*

Limits need not apply only to what you spend. Limiting how quickly you close a deal often can be very useful. If you are shopping for an underground sprinkler system, for example, you may want to decide beforehand that no purchase will be made today. Instead, you will wait at least one or two days, or perhaps longer, before continuing the negotiation. After all, you can explain, you have to check with your husband (wife, partner) before making a final decision. This gives you time to think again about the product, the price, and the provider. During the interim, do not be surprised if the other party to the negotiation calls, which tells you something about his desire to close the deal.

Rehearse

Negotiations seldom follow a script. They are fluid, discontinuous, generally unpredictable processes. Nonetheless, it can be useful to think, before a face-to-face encounter, about the three questions presented in Chapter 3, and to visualize how you might approach the other party. How can you help them or hurt them (that is, what are their problems or needs)? What are some questions they are likely to ask? How will you respond? If you are going for a job interview, there are certain questions that many recruiters like to ask (for example, "What are your strengths?" "Describe one weakness" "Where would you like to be in five years?").

*Gaming houses or casinos prefer that you have no idea how much money you are losing, so they have you buy chips or tokens to play with rather than cold, hard cash. This way, you always get something for your money: the playing chips.

As the epigraph from Paul Simon at the beginning of Chapter 3 suggests, improvisation is too good to leave to chance. Think about the strategy or tactics to employ. If you are going to use one of the tactics presented earlier, such as good guy, bad guy, you at least want to know who is playing which role. If the negotiation is sufficiently valuable, you may want to role-play in advance. Law firms do this before major court cases. Businesses do this before making sales presentations.

Suppose, for example, that you are a businessperson preparing to pitch a new product or service. You might want to practice your presentation in front of a friend or colleague, or videotape yourself. To get the real flavor of the give-and-take of a negotiation, pick a company that you do *not* expect to be your primary buyer or client and practice your negotiating skills at this site rather than with the primary company with whom you expect to complete your negotiations. It gives you a feel for the issues, the industry, the market, and your readiness. You will be better informed and have more confidence when the time comes to approach your target company.

Use an Agent

Despite Claudio's admonition in Shakespeare's *Much Ado About Nothing*—"Let every eye negotiate for itself, And trust no agent" (Act II, Scene 1, 185)—there are many times when a trusted agent is well advised (*trusted* being the operative word here, as Myles Standish discovered in sending John Alden to inquire about Priscilla Mullins).

We initiate negotiations because we want something. The more valuable it is to us, the more hurt, disappointed, frustrated, or angry we are likely to feel if we do not get it. Even a good negotiator can give away the store out of fear of losing something of great emotional value. In such situations, finding someone who can negotiate on your behalf—an agent—is often one of the best things you can do.

One advantage that a negotiating agent possesses over his "client" is that he has little or no emotional baggage. The other party in a negotiation can often sense the value that an agreement has for you and take advantage of this information. An agent is not as apt to show frustration, anger, anxiety, or desire.

At one stage in my career, I was developing software to help people who run meetings understand the problems they are having and manage their meetings more effectively and efficiently. I did not know the publishing business, yet I tried to represent myself in finding a company to sell the software. This was "my baby," and I did not want to lose control of the idea, the product, or the process. The publishing organization that eventually agreed to carry the software was relatively small. I dealt with a representative of the organization, not the president (who made the final decision). At one point, after going to lunch at a nice restaurant, the representative suggested that if the software sold well, I might have my own table at the restaurant someday. I beamed, a reaction that undoubtedly was not lost on him. He was playing on my desire to be a success.

Using an agent in a business negotiation also communicates something about the legitimacy of your enterprise. Alexandre Silva, president of a Brazilian company called Celma that rebuilds turbojet engines, described how his company attempted to develop contracts with North American companies through meetings in the United States. Silva and one or two associates arranged the meetings and represented Celma themselves. Nothing came of it. His company had no credibility, and even though he spoke English it was (and is) difficult to negotiate across cultures. So he hired a North American agent, and before long they began to get some contracts.

When you go to buy a house, do you feel more comfortable if the seller is representing himself, or if he has a real estate agent? If you are like most people, you would rather have an agent involved, even though the agent is technically representing the seller! It seems more legitimate. (By the way, there are now buyer agents for home purchasers as well.)

Beyond legitimacy, an agent can simply pretend not to know if he or she has information that is best not divulged at this time (the playing-dumb tactic). In addition, an agent can say things in a negotiation that you might not be able to say yourself (for example, tough talk), including things for which you do not want to be held accountable. Much as in a courtroom, where a defense lawyer is professionally dressed, articulate, and at times ruthless in pursuit of an advantage, you are not held fully responsible for your agent's behavior. When Johnny Cochran "played the race card" in the O.J. Simpson murder trial, we probably did not think any less of Simpson for these accusations. However, we might have if Simpson himself had accused the Los Angeles Police Department of being racist. Therefore, you can be the good guy (and the agent the bad guy) in an implicit good-guy, bad-guy situation.

Be advised that some lawyers are risk-averse by profession (remember the Five-Minute University and the one-minute law school, where "Never ask a question to which you do not already know the answer" is all that is taught). As advisers, they may see a problem in every proposal and generate more conflicts than they resolve. Furthermore, using an agent requires not only that you be able to answer that initial fundamental question—*What do I want?*—for yourself but that you communicate this to your representative as well. A good agent, however, helps you in clarifying your positions and interests.

18

Personal Action Plan

Few things are impossible to diligence and skill.
—Samuel Johnson

George Nelson tells a story of his mentor, Frank Lloyd Wright, who began to muse about architecture while the two were taking a walk. Wright was trying to capture the essence of architecture in a single phrase or image. What *is* this endeavor that has become his life's work? Seeing a flower, Wright drew a comparison, suggesting that architecture was like a flower. Then he paused and withdrew the analogy. Walking a bit farther, Wright made a second comparison that suited him better: Architecture is like love.

There are many ways of interpreting this simile. One is to recognize that both architecture and love are art forms. There is no template for success. What worked last week might not work this week under "the same," or different, conditions. Like a relationship, architecture is constantly evolving. One must be constantly adapting and learning, as well.

The same can be said of negotiation. Negotiation is an art form. Sometimes the approach that worked last week doesn't work this time. However, there are some basic skills of negotiating just as there are some basic tenets of architecture and love. As skills, these tenets must be practiced to be acquired, and practiced again if we are to remain sharp in their nuance. This is true of all art forms. It is why Tiger Woods continues to take golf lessons and practice his craft, why mezzo-soprano Cecilia Bartoli continues to take voice direction, and why Harvey Keitel still employs a coach before and during the making of a film.

Unless you have skipped forward to this final section of the book, which is not advised, you now know a lot more about yourself and negotiation than you did at the beginning. In addition, you have been able to practice some new behaviors and tactics that will help you become more effective in the art of social and business negotiation.

You probably recognize that you have some special competencies as a negotiator, as well as some areas that could use further development. As a way of tying together what you have observed and learned in going through this book, complete the following self-assessment, identifying your competencies and those areas where you need to change, improve, or develop.

Let's begin with your special competencies or skills. On the lines below, describe five skills that represent your special negotiation competencies. Be *very* specific in your responses, citing behaviors (such as testing understanding or summarizing discussions), tactics (silence, authority limits), countermeasures (responding to speed-ups and delays), flexibility, creativity, type of negotiations, etc., that you feel are your strengths.

a. _____

b. _____

c. _____

d. _____

e. _____

Now list five negotiation skills that you feel you need to change, improve, or develop. Again, be very specific and descriptive in your responses, including the circumstances under which difficulties occur ("explaining my reasoning before disagreeing, especially when dealing with my subordinates at work").

a. _____

b. _____

c. _____

d. _____

e. _____

In the latter list of skills (the ones that you feel you need to change, improve, or develop), rank the five in order of importance (that is, prioritize the list), assigning 1 to the skill that you most need to develop, 2 to the second most important, etc.

The final step in this process is to think about how you are going to acquire these skills and develop a personal action plan. Let's focus on your top priority. Write this skill on the next page, and describe five things that you can do to acquire it. Be as specific as possible, indicating activities, people who will help you, and a timetable for your development. Think about how you might involve your spouse, family, and friends in this process. They probably already know many of your competencies as well as where you need further development. How often per week can you practice? For how many weeks? How do you know that you are making progress?

Suppose, for example, that one of the skills you most need to work on is asking open-ended questions, particularly at the beginning of a negotiation. You might plan to practice this at least once a day, starting with something simple such as asking "What did you have in mind?" or "What kind of food were you thinking of?" when a colleague comes to your office to ask you to go to lunch. You might tell your significant other that you are working on acquiring this behavior, and ask for suggestions as to when you might use it more effectively with him or her. Then, commit yourself to doing so at least twice per week, requesting feedback from your significant other every week or two. Gradually progress to more difficult situations, such as when subordinates ask for favors or your boss gives you an assignment. You might even keep a chart of your progress, noting which questions seem to work better than others.

Do you get the idea? The more detail you put into your personal action plan, the better. This is a working document.

PERSONAL ACTION PLAN

Top-priority skill: _____

_____

Specific activities:

1. _____

   _____

2. _____

   _____

3. _____

   _____

4. _____

   _____

5. _____

   _____

Timetable:

|-------------------- |-------------------- |------------------ |------------------ |------------------ |

Epilogue

A bit of fragrance clings to the hand that gives the flower.

—Chinese proverb

Congratulations!

With all the demands on your time and life's many distractions, you have nonetheless completed the challenge. You have finished this book, and in the process you have discovered myriad things about yourself—including your risk-taking propensity, negotiating style, and ethics. You have gained some valuable insights into those individuals with whom you regularly negotiate, at home and at work. In addition, you have practiced a half dozen or more negotiations, and learned some new behaviors, tactics, and countermeasures.

You now know more about preparing for negotiations and how to close a deal and record an agreement than you did a hundred-plus pages ago. In fact, if you haven't done this already you might want to compare the feedback from an earlier negotiation (Valero Wine–Continental Glass, Chapter 6) with the feedback from your final one (Logan Telecommunications–RJW Properties, Chapter 16) to see just how much progress you have made.

Without question, you are a lot better at negotiating than you realize. You always were. After all, you have been negotiating for your entire life, beginning from infancy, when you wanted to be fed or held, to when you first asked to stay up past midnight on New Year's Eve, to picking which movie to see with a friend last weekend. You were negotiating—communicating with another person to determine the nature of future behavior, as I defined it in Chapter 1. You just didn't realize it.

Given your years of experience as a negotiator, this book has sought to help you bring your best skills to the fore. You have gifts; recognize them and use them. At the same time, there are probably some new techniques and behaviors that you want to add to your repertoire. With practice, these too will become second nature to you.

The vast majority of your daily negotiations can seem inconsequential. Whether you lunch with a friend at an Italian restaurant or a Mexican restaurant, and whether you meet there at noon or twelve-thirty, makes little difference in the grand scheme of things. In another sense, however, these daily negotiations constitute your training ground. They are dress rehearsals, of sorts. How you handle these everyday negotiations is likely to mirror how you approach the more important and challenging negotiations that are less frequently encountered—an automobile sale, a home acquisition, a new job offer. So think about incorporating your new tactics and behaviors into your everyday negotiations, and you will feel more comfortable and confident in using them when these less-frequent but more-momentous negotiations arise.

Many examples and case simulations have been used throughout this book to introduce specific points about negotiation. Yet the process of negotiation is far more continuous than episodic. You are always negotiating. Even when you sign an agreement, negotiating may not end. Virtually everything is negotiable, and virtually everything involves negotiation. Negotiation is part of the ongoing flow of life, and your reputation or persona is tightly interwoven with your interpersonal encounters and success. You want to feel good about your negotiations, and you want other parties to feel good about their interactions with you as well. You want your counterparts to look forward to negotiating with you again, and to speak well of you to others (which constitutes a first step in your negotiation with them).

The more challenging and demanding that life's negotiations become, the more you need to attend to fundamentals. And there is nothing more fundamental than our Golden Rule of negotiation. People negotiate with you if they believe you can help them or hurt them. How can you help the other party? If you can keep your focus on answering this question, you will do just fine. In addition, as the quotation that introduces this final chapter suggests, you will come out smelling like a rose.

Appendix A

Continental Glass
(Confidential Facts)

You represent a glass-manufacturing company called Continental Glass. Your company is a relatively new player in what is otherwise a well-established industry. Continental makes a variety of glass products but is primarily into wholesale bottle manufacture for beverages of all types.

Currently, your inventory is overstocked with a small, 100-ml bottle sometimes used in the airline industry, and a very large bottle (jug) that has not sold well in recent years. You have 120,000 of the small, 100-ml bottles in stock because a distributor to the airline industry declared bankruptcy after you agreed to manufacture the bottle. You have been carrying these bottles for almost six months, and the other primary distributor has not shown the same interest because of a potential change in airline policy.

Valero Wine Company has made an inquiry about a smaller-than-normal bottle, which it refers to as gift-sized. You are about to meet with a representative of Valero Wine, and you would really like to unload the 100-ml bottles. But you would also like to develop a long-term relationship. Here are some facts to help you with the negotiation:

1. It cost you 10 cents per bottle to manufacture the 120,000 100-ml bottles.
2. To make a profit, you need to sell a bottle of this type for at least 15 cents per bottle.
3. A rush order generally is anything less than two weeks, and you charge an additional 5 cents per bottle for rush orders.

4. The recycling value of the bottles is about 5 cents per bottle.

As you meet with the representative of Valero Wine, keep in mind that your goal is to sell all 120,000 for the best price possible.

Appendix B
Sales Manager, Carson Enterprises (Confidential Facts)

You are the director of sales for a publishing company called Carson Enterprises, whose primary product is a monthly magazine. The company was originally a family-owned business, but it is now publicly owned. The sales force at Carson consists of seven people, only one of whom has been with the company more than three years. Over the years, the company has seen good times and bad times. Generally speaking, as the economy goes, so goes Carson Enterprises. This is because the company is largely dependent upon advertising revenue, and a poor economy almost invariably leads to a decline in advertisers, the size of their ads, or the frequency of their ads. At the moment, the economy appears to be a bit uncertain.

The salespeople at Carson work on a salary-plus-commission basis. The salary is usually between $40,000 and $50,000, depending on how long the individual has been with the company. The commission is between 2 and 3 percent of each sale, for all sales beyond $1 million. Again, the rate of the commission depends upon the years of service the salesperson has with the company, and how much he or she brings in. Each salesperson has his or her own client base, and some client bases are better than others.

One of the two salespeople that you hired within the past year has asked for a meeting to talk about a six-month performance review (and, most likely, a salary adjustment). You would like to keep this salesperson, who has been with Carson six or seven months and looks to have promise. So far, this salesperson has brought in close to $700,000. However, given the uncertainty of the economy, you need to be careful about giving too big a raise. Also, you don't want this to get around to the other salespeople and be faced with other demands for a salary adjustment, either base or commission.

You have two roles in this negotiation simulation. The first, of course, is to play the role of the director of sales at Carson Enterprises. Play this role in whatever way feels comfortable to you, given the background information above. The second role is to provide some tactical challenges to the person who has asked you to help him or her with this simulation: the salesperson who is about to come to you with a request for a six-month performance review and a salary increase (base, commission, or both). This individual will indicate which tactics he or she needs practice in handling. Read over the suggestions for how to approach each of the tactics checked below, and think about how you might work them into your negotiation. You don't have to use all of them, but pick at least three or four. Some of these tactics work best at the beginning of the negotiation (for example, an exaggerated first offer), whereas others make more sense at the end (for example, authority limits).

_____ 1. Exaggerated first offer: You make the first offer, a $200 increase in monthly base salary and no commission increase.

_____ 2. Speed-ups: Say that you are in a hurry (important meeting upcoming) and would like to conclude this negotiation within five minutes.

_____ 3. Delays: Ask if you can get back to this person next week; ask to do an eighteen-month performance evaluation instead.

_____ 4. Drawing lines: Say immediately that you cannot discuss performance evaluation, because this is being revamped by the company.

_____ 5. Concessions: Regardless of how this person responds to your offer, concede only marginal adjustments (for example, increase your base-salary offer by $100 or less).

_____ 6. Creating competition: Indicate that this morning you received three unsolicited calls from highly qualified people looking for a sales position with the company.

_____ 7. Investment: Spend a lot of time with this person, talking about everything but the issue (family, sports, etc.); suggest going to get something to eat together.

_____ 8. Authority limits: Once you get an agreement, indicate that you must check with the vice president for marketing and sales.

_____ 9. Silence: Say very little; ask the other party to tell you more.

_____10. Playing dumb: Pretend that you don't know what this person is talking about regarding a six-month performance review.

_____11. Playing the crazy: Pretend to be in a frenzy, or react with strong emotion (surprise, disappointment) to this person's offer.

_____12. Showing off the goods: Show this person sales numbers indicating a downward trend.

_____13. Flattery: Call this person by his or her first name; comment positively on something he or she is wearing.

_____14. Buying your objections: For every concern or issue this person raises besides more money, say, "We can fix that."

_____15. Lowballing: Mention that all the other publishers you know of start out at $30,000 and 1.5 percent commission.

_____16. Strawman: Mention that there is a parking shortage at the company; offer a parking spot in return for lower salary or lower commission.

_____17. Bundling: Once an agreement has been determined, add on a condition that the individual offer some sales training for incoming staff.

_____18. Confederates: Announce that three other people are on their way to join you in the negotiation.

_____19. Good guy, bad guy: Pretend that the vice president for marketing and sales has been talking about reducing the commission structure; say that you would like to keep it as is.

_____20. Split the difference: When you get near a final agreement on base or commission, suggest a compromise by splitting the difference between your positions.

Appendix C
RJW Properties, Inc.
(Confidential Facts)

You represent a company called RJW Properties that buys, sells, leases, and manages commercial properties. RJW Properties has been in the real estate business more than thirty years and currently handles nearly two dozen properties in the area.

A representative from a company called Logan Telecommunications is interested in leasing a 3,000 square foot commercial space in one of your buildings. This building is in a very good location for commercial development, and it comes with some parking space. Despite the location, the real estate market has been sluggish for the past two years and this particular property has been vacant for six months. You would like to lease it, preferably under a long-term contract (three- or four-year lease).

Although the length of the lease is an important issue for you, there are, in fact, at least seven issues that have to be resolved to complete this negotiation:

1. Cost per square foot
2. Renovation of space
3. Utilities
4. Length of lease
5. Parking
6. Furnishings
7. Advanced payment

For each of these issues, there are several possible outcomes. For each outcome that you negotiate, you receive a specific number of points. These points reflect how important the issue and outcome are to you and your company. These are shown in the Scoring Key that follows.

Your counterpart at Logan Telecommunications has his or her own scoring key, which is different from yours. Do not share your scoring key with him or her, because this is confidential information. Once you have completed your negotiation, record your agreement on the form that follows your scoring key; both of you must sign the agreement form. Your goal is to negotiate the highest score possible.

Scoring Key for RJW Properties, Inc.

Issue	Negotiated Outcome	Point Value
Cost per square foot	$50	300
	$60	450
	$70	600
	$80	750
	$90	900
Renovation of space	No rooms renovated	550
	One room	300
	Two rooms	200
	Three rooms	150
Utilities included	None	300
	Water and sewer	150
	Water, sewer, and electricity	100
Length of lease	One year	200
	Two years	500
	Three years	700
	Four years	900
Parking available	No cars	300
	One car	250
	Two cars	200
	Three cars	150
	Four cars	100

Appendix C: RJW Properties Inc.

Issue	Negotiated Outcome	Point Value
Furnishings	None	150
	Refrigerator and stove	150
Advanced payment	One month's rent	200
	Six months' rent	600
	One year's rent	900

RJW Properties, Inc.
Commercial Property Leasing Contract

Issue	Terms
Cost per square foot	_____
Renovation of space	_____
Utilities	_____
Length of lease	_____
Parking	_____
Furnishings	_____
Advanced payment	_____

_____
Logan Telecommunications
Representative (signature)

_____
RJW Properties, Inc.
Representative (signature)

Resources

Books

Acuff, F. L. *How to Negotiate Anything With Anyone Anywhere Around the World*. New York: AMACOM, 1997.

Adler, N. J. *International Dimensions of Organizational Behavior* (3rd ed.). Cincinnati: South-Western, 1997.

Cohen, H. *You Can Negotiate Anything*. New York: Bantam Books, 1980.

Farson, R. *Management of the Absurd: Paradoxes of Leadership*. New York: Simon & Schuster, 1996.

Fisher, R., Ury, W., and Patton, B. *Getting to Yes: Negotiating Agreement Without Giving In*. New York: Penguin Books, 1991.

Foster, D. A. *Bargaining Across Borders: How to Negotiate Business Successfully Anywhere in the World*. New York: McGraw-Hill, 1992.

Hendon, D. W., Hendon, R. A., and Herbig, P. *Cross-Cultural Business Negotiations*. Westport, Ct.: Quorum Books, 1996.

Keltner, J. W. *The Management of Struggle: Elements of Dispute Resolution Through Negotiation, Mediation, and Arbitration*. Cresskill, N.J.: Hampton Press, 1994.

Lax, D. A., and Sebenius, J. K. *The Manager as Negotiator: Bargaining for Cooperation and Competitive Gain*. New York: Free Press, 1986.

Lewicki, R. J., Saunders, D. M., and Minton, J. W. *Essentials of Negotiation*. Burr Ridge, Ill.: Irwin, 1997.

MacCrimmon, K. R., and Wehrung, D. A. *Taking Risks: The Management of Uncertainty*. New York: Free Press, 1986.

Morrison, T., Conaway, W. A., and Borden, G. A. *Kiss, Bow, or Shake Hands: How to Do Business in Sixty Countries*. Holbrook, Mass.: Adams Media, 1994.

Rackham, N. "The Behavior of Successful Negotiators." In R. L. Lewicki, J. A. Litterer, D. M. Saunders, and J. W. Minton (eds.), *Negotiation: Readings, Exercises, and Cases* (3rd ed.). Burr Ridge, Ill.: Irwin, 1999.

Rubin, J. Z., and Brown, B. R. *The Social Psychology of Bargaining and Negotiation.* New York: Academic Press, 1975.

Schatzki, M. *Negotiation: The Art of Getting What You Want.* New York: Signet, 1981.

Schuster, C., and Copeland, M. *Global Business: Planning for Sales and Negotiations.* Fort Worth: Dryden, 1996.

Videos

"The Abilene Paradox." CRM Productions, Carlsbad, CA 92008. 1984. (27 minutes). Also, a book: Harvey, J. *The Abilene Paradox and Other Meditations on Management.* Lexington, MA.: Lexington Books, 1988.

"The Car Buyer's Survival Guide." John Spiropoulos and John Harter, Information Videos. 1991. (42 minutes).

"Managing Your Boss." MTI Film & Video (Simon & Schuster), 420 Academy Dr., Northbrook, IL 60062. 1986. (32 minutes).

"Mediation in Action: Resolving a Complex Business Dispute." CPR Institute for Dispute Resolution, New York, NY. 1994. (36 minutes).

"Meetings, Bloody Meetings." Video Arts, 8614 West Catalpa, Chicago, IL 60656. 1993. (35 minutes).

"Negotiating." American Management Association, Nine Galen Street, Watertown, MA 02172. 1994. (28 minutes).

Contracts on the World Wide Web

www.procopio.com/Resources/Bus_Info/businfo.htm

* Promissory note (variable rate)
* Proprietary information and inventions agreement for independent contractors

- Stock restriction agreement
- Independent contractor's agreement
- Agreement with respect to the exchange of proprietary data

www.legaldocs.com

- Partnership agreements
- Office leases
- Nondisclosure agreements
- Bill of sale
- Rental agreement
- Power of attorney
- Employment agreement

www.youngartists.com/contract.htm

- Young artists' galley sales contract
- Transfer agreement and record
- Statement of maintenance
- Bill of sale

Index